WHEN THE EXTREME RIGHT
IS EXTREMELY WRONG

by

Luis Fernando Gutierrez

Order this book online at www.trafford.com
or email orders@trafford.com

Most Trafford titles are also available at major online book retailers.

Print information available on the last page.

ISBN: 978-1-5536-9165-5 (sc)

Trafford rev. 06/27/2022

Trafford
PUBLISHING® www.trafford.com
North America & international
toll-free: 844-688-6899 (USA & Canada)
fax: 812 355 4082

DEDICATION

This book is dedicated first and foremost to the One True God (Yahweh) – and our Messiah Jesus Christ (Yeshua) who has been wrongfully portrayed throughout the centuries as a conservative-rightist by the traditionally rightist-conservative Holy Roman Catholic Church. May those who read it concur that its primary source, the 66 books which make up the modern version of the Judeo-Christian Bible, are as equally balanced as is God Almighty. The scriptures are actually of more value to humanity today than ever before, as many hidden revelations within the prophetic books have been revealed to man in recent times. The overriding theme of recognizing "extremely wrong" scriptural perception, interpretation, and projection may be of interest to some of even other faiths. The time and effort spent on this work is also dedicated to my family, the modest liberal, and the masses of genuinely good spirited people, including many conservatives, who have struggled with the monumental evil of both extremes, particularly the extreme right.

CONTENTS

Note: Since this book is based on Biblical principles, various excerpts are quoted directly from the King James Revised-Standard Bible, while others are only mentioned. However, one can clearly understand the inherent messages without having to refer to the Bible. It is never-the-less recommended that the reader have a Bible handy, as it is ultimately the scriptures which speak for themselves.

INTRODUCTION

The erroneous perception which too many people have of the Heavenly Father and our Messiah, Jesus Christ, is what fervently stirs inside me the desire to bring about a more balanced view of them. In doing so, the spiritual / religious origins of what constitutes "rightist" and "leftist" philosophy must be integrated into the political arena in order to bring about the intended objective: to prove beyond a shadow of a doubt that like Christ, his Father is not the "conservative" deity that many would assume (among other vital issues). Some believe that since Christ will return *"seated at the right hand of power,"* (Matthew 26:64), he is some sort of right-wing Messiah. It is clear to me that some may be inclined to conclude that this work is an evil deed, while others may feel that this more balanced reasoning of the profile of God, Christ, and the scriptures is long overdue. Needless to say, the contents of this writing are geared toward the latter. I believe this group is considerable in number and not limited to one geographic zone. Since evil prevails when good people do nothing and bad people are busy doing their wicked deeds, it is necessary to re-emphasize some fundamental Biblical principles. It is my objective to highlight some key social issues from a modestly liberal perspective with a dash of conservatism for balance. This approach is intended as a "breath of fresh air," shedding new light for this new world and its "new age" policies.

To those who may feel that this work is blasphemous, heretical, or evil, I would only like to remind them that these claims, among others, were made of not only Christ (ie: John 8:49; John 15:18) and the disciples, but of his true followers. In that sense, it would be a compliment to me. Christ was perceived by many as being a religious zealot, a false prophet, an impersonator, strange, peculiar, and out of touch with this world. He was oftentimes the butt of jokes, ridiculed, mocked, and treated as a lunatic by the strict and hard right due, in part, to his numerous messages which had a liberal connotation (Mark 14:65 and 15:29-32, Luke 23:11).

The cliche "right is right and wrong is wrong" is one which is not consistent with this work, for it is my intention to prove that quite often the right is quite wrong. This does not imply that conservative ideology is all bad, but that mankind often takes matters too far to either extreme, thus, we err – boy, do we err! In various ways, I myself lean to the moderate right as is necessary to thwart the wickedness which is at the extreme left, although not autonomous, in that it is increasingly manipulated by the Far-Right.

For quite some time, I have been perplexed by the way in which many seem to assert a one-sided, right-wing ideology as it applies to The Father, Christ, their teachings, and the scriptures. Clearly, History, "his" story, or man's fallible records of the past and the false and misleading perceptions passed on through the centuries, has promoted a rather conservative Christ through the eyes of the Catholic Church. Many of those who have protested much of the Church's dogma have continued to reveal a solely conservative Messiah.

Matter, place, and time (the human, the homeland, and the Hebrew time-clock) have been increasingly the primary targets of the demonic realm. As a result, I intend to elaborate as to how Satan, by way of the Far-Right particularly, will continue to be on the offensive against God and Christ. This self-righteous right actually had the audacity to alter God's word in numerous ways. This is the utmost of blasphemies. The rhetoric of the Church's beliefs and customs became of gargantuan proportions, as they changed the Ten Commandments to suit their idolatrous ways and a Satanic timeframe. The second commandment has been omitted, the fourth altered, and the tenth divided in two (Exodus 20).

THE COMMANDMENTS OF GOD ALMIGHTY
(EXODUS 20)
1. *Thou shall have no other gods before Me.*
2. *Thou shall not make for yourself any graven image.*
3. *Thou shall not take the name of the Lord your God in vain.*
4. *Remember the Sabbath day.*
5. *Honor thy Father and Mother.*

6. *Thou shall not kill.*
7. *Thou shall not commit adultery.*
8. *Thou shall not steal.*
9. *Thou shall not bear false witness.*
10. *Thou shall not covet anything that belongs to thy neighbor.*

THE COMMANDMENTS AS CHANGED BY THE VATICAN (CATECHISM)
1. *Thou shall not have strange gods before Me.*
2. *Thou shall not use the Lord's name in vain.*
3. *Remember that thou keep holy the Sabbath day.*
4. *Honor thy Father and Mother.*
5. *Thou shall not kill.*
6. *Thou shall not commit adultery.*
7. *Thou shall not steal.*
8. *Thou shall not bear false witness.*
9. *Thou shall not covet thy neighbor's wife.*
10. *Thou shall not covet thy neighbor's goods.*

In Matthew 19:16-19, Christ is clearly giving the Ten Commandments great emphasis in responding to a man who came along asking him what God required a person do in order to enter the kingdom. He certainly did not change any of them in the least, nor did he discard them as being null and void.

Taking an in depth look at the Ten Commandments being promoted by the Religious Right will leave one mesmerized by seeing who is ultimately behind this. The first and second commandments, as we will see later, are today as critical for God as they were yesterday. Not only has Rome claimed to have authority to interpret the scriptures but to actually change them by adding or deleting to the word. Deuteronomy 4:2, *"You shall not add to the word which I command you, nor take from it; that you may keep the commandments of the Lord your God which I command you."* See also Revelations 22:18-19. In addition, the Catholic Church has actually claimed the right to damn and curse anyone who opposes it by not following its "divine authority." This offensive and startling position is more than a mere gesture of disagreement, it threatens to do what only God has ultimate authority to do – to judge, condemn, and castigate an individual for not heeding his call. Too often though, today's Rome is perceived as being solely a thing of the past, taken with a grain of salt, out-dated, dull, and overly ceremonial. This brings a sense of apathy by the masses regarding the Church's influence over their lives. The notion that Church and State are indeed separate does not help any either – a hot issue we will explore later. Since God is the same yesterday, today, and tomorrow, a conservative attribute, in that he does not change (Malachi 3:6), then for Babylonian-Rome to change one iota of the sacred scriptures is a severe and catastrophic conflict of interest.

Some assert that Christ came to change the law and that in doing so, he demonstrated that God does indeed change. However, Christ did not come to change the law itself, he came "to fulfil" it, as had been prophesied in the Old Testament; moreover, whoever even relaxes any of the commandments is "skating on thin ice" – Matthew 5:17-20; Luke16:17. In Luke 5:14, Christ is instructing the leper which he just healed to, *"make an offering for your cleansing as Moses commanded."* 1 John 3:4 says, *"sin is the transgression of the law."* Jeremiah 31:31 foretold of "The New Covenant" which would be fulfilled by Christ. Though superior to the first, this new covenant remains an extension of the old. Hebrews 8:6-7 says, *"But as it is, Christ has obtained a ministry which is as much more excellent than the old as the covenant he mediates is better, since it is enacted on better promises. For if that first covenant had been faultless, there would have been no occasion for a second."* This could be summed up in deducing that the Messiah Christ did away with the "legalism" (ie: blood / animal sacrifices) of the law, not the foundation of the law which embraced, both then and now, those who accept it.

One of my all time favorite excerpts which get to "the bottom line" of the reasons why Christ came to this world (and incidentally, the true essence of this writing) is depicted in Matthew 23:23. Here, Christ is protesting the manner in which the legalistic Scribes and Pharisees (associates / members of the elitist Sanhedrin Court) were unjust, merciless, and unfaithful. It was these "wise men" who, by their hard-line conservative nature, continuously "pointed fingers" and challenged Christ's ethics, morals, and spirituality. Luke 6:42, *"Or how can you say to your brother, 'Brother, let me take out the speck that is in your eye,' when you yourselves do not see the log that is in your eye?"* It is as clear as daylight that many of Christ's conflicts in law were with the Far-Right. Then, as today, they held the same principles of conduct – being constantly critical of others, absorbed by their self-righteousness, and quick to condemn anyone as though they are "righteous." We should never lose sight of the fact that Christ and his disciples were martyred by the Roman legal system and some who claimed to be Jews. Christ came, in part, to make it clear that it is the "weightier matters" which will be of real importance throughout time. Thus, "the last days," will be our last chance to focus on what really matters: being "just, merciful, and faithful." On the great and final judgement day, we will be judged by the more crucial and vitally humane issues which emanate from this foundation.

Christ would most certainly not fall under the commonly held view of a rightist- conservative. He is the perfect blend of left and right, thus, one should never attempt to label him as either, for he is neither of the two. To stereotype him as a right-winger or necessarily conservative is blasphemous. Those who do are inherently in conflict with many of the principles which he taught and the morals within his liberal messages and parables.

To repair the numerous breaches which have been integrated into the teachings of the Church for so long will take much more than this work, but hopefully a seed will be planted so the result will cause some to thoroughly question the extremes, in particular the self-righteous-right which is dangerously on the rise again. Various sources within the Protestant movement have touched on a few of the "revelations" mentioned in this writing and are subsequently credited at the end of each chapter where appropriate. However, no writing has taken a viewpoint quite like this – from "the Bible's political profile" to "abortion" to "the drug war" to "the mark of the beast" to the outwardly "centrist" Anti- Christ and New World Order and beyond.

This is not a self-righteous, pompous, or judgmental composition, as I am not writing it out of conceit or a belief that I am a genius, prophet, or teacher. Instead, I write as a sort of modestly liberal servant (with some conservative views), albeit a sinner none- the- less, with a timely message for the masses. I am not claiming to be on equal grounds with any Biblical writer, merely following up on much of their "heavenly work" as it applies to a series of extremely important issues in this day and new age. It is with a sincere devotion to the Utopia which is God Almighty, whom I most earnestly serve by bringing to the forefront the fact that the celestial body is not necessarily conservative, among many other relevant issues. Thus, "the other side of the coin" is the main focus of this writing.

Success to me is measured by humble servitude to God, enlightenment and brotherly love one brings to others, and total dedication to those weightier matters of life mentioned above. The consciousness I wish to raise via what is entailed in this book is one of great benefit to the spiritual realm of our existence. It is the modern-day political arena which is "under a microscope" and even more-so, the Judeo-Christian Bible which is being put under great scrutiny as 1 Thessalonians 5:19-21 suggests doing. Therefore, my intention is to bring a heightened awareness of the scriptures from a modestly liberal interpretation, as they apply to a variety of hotly-debated issues today.

At the time of this writing, this nation is entering a new war which could last for many years and involve many countries in the long run. Much of the world will be initially confronting primarily the Islamic extremists and their extremist interpretation of the Koran, as it is these who validate mass murder in the name of Allah. Though I cannot rationalize this sort of spirituality, I sympathize with many good Muslims throughout the world who are paying a dear price for merely being who they are. Extremist interpretation of any religious doctrine is what compels me to bring to light how the Bible will be, as prophesied, used by other extremists, the "Globalists"- Satan's disciples, who also come "in the name of God / Christ" to establish their New World Order.

As to this writing, it is imperative to make some things very clear: 1) It is not critical of Catholic people, of which many of my own family members are, or of the genuine goodness of many of the

Church's clergy world-wide, but it does pierce through the veil of the contradictory Catholic hierarchy, doctrine, and rituals; 2) It gives a great deal of credit to much of the Protestant movement for its part in history, particularly a variety of "Sabbath keeping" churches for going one step further in their protest. Hence, this work is not critical of Protestant people either, but it does reveal some stimulating discrepancies with their mostly conservative interpretation of scripture, among other issues. Thus, I do not necessarily adhere to any one denomination. Though I am not a very "religious" man, my root beliefs are synonymous with the first "Christian Church" which was founded by Christ himself and his disciples; 3) It is mildly inclined to the left in order to create the balance needed in addressing the Far-Right; 4) It sincerely applauds the inclusiveness of all peoples, though not all "gods." Again, I cannot over-emphasize the first and second commandments; 5) It is not biased toward any race, culture, or people, but it is realistic in concluding that not all Europeans are the "good guys;" 6) It does not attempt to label Christ in any way whatsoever, nor is it my contention that he was necessarily a pacifist; 7) It is certainly not anti-Semitic, but is realistic in recognizing that not all "Jews" are of the Synagogues of God; 8) It is not on the offensive – quite the contrary, it is on the defensive; 9) It honors the integrity of the U.S. legal system as the finest in this world. Because dissent is patriotic and necessary in a democracy, as it brings to light one's views of how to improve society, I primarily disagree with various high- profile conservative points; 10) It shows why it is a flaw to conclude that there are no conspiracies in anything, without concluding that there is a conspiracy in everything. Satan, having mastered the art of conspiring long ago, is who continues his wicked conspiracies against mankind in order to avenge his "eviction" from the heavens; 11) It thoroughly puts into perspective the fact that some of what we consider myth is not myth at all – it is actually true; 12) It addresses religious, political, and social issues as they apply on a local as well as global level – because what happens in one neighborhood can affect another half-way around the world.

✻   ✻   ✻   ✻   ✻   ✻   ✻

CHAPTER ONE

THE CONSERVATIVE CHURCH
AND ITS HOLIDAYS

Having a Catholic upbringing, I was taught early on to follow the teachings of the Roman Catholic Church with all its rituals and idolatry. Not knowing any better, I prayed to the array of idols common to every Catholic around the world. I perceived the barrage of statues and monuments of Mary and the saints to be an integral part of being spiritual and godly. I was immersed in the pagan ways of this worldwide entity which prized itself on being the ultimate authority on the interpretation of scripture and as being the head of Christ on earth until his dramatic return.

For decades, some very fundamental questions remained unanswered for me and it has been a true challenge sifting through a substantial amount of literature (ironically, much of it conservative) and discerning with the scriptures what really is the truth Christ referred to which would set us "free." Recognizing this freedom, I was able to see what is Satan-inspired / man-made doctrine which conversely, keeps us in bondage. Realizing that the history of the rightist-Vatican is plagued with major conflicts between what it says and what it does, as was clear during the reign of Adolf Hitler, I sensed a need to better understand the "truths" behind what the hierarchy teaches the masses to blindly follow without questioning its authority. It is interesting how the cross, which is the universal symbol of Christ brought to us by the Church, was revised by the more radical Nazi's. Swastika: an ancient design in the form of a cross with arms of equal length bent in a right angle. Although the Church has had to make major changes to its rightist- ideology, in part as a result of inner struggles pulling it toward the center-left and in order to appear as distant in overall policy from the Church of yesterday, the essence of an inclination to the Far-Right has not and will not be lost.

All those who, in the name of righteousness, perished during WWII because of the blatant racism of Hitler, I acknowledge as true heroes and martyrs who have spilled their blood in battles against extreme evil. These should be remembered and honored by every American, even more-so by Jews, Jehovah's Witnesses, homosexuals, and others who were targets and victims of the Far-Right. On this note, I would like to relay a message of sincere condolence and appreciation to all veterans and those missing in action / prisoners of war. They are oftentimes short-changed by big government, as many have to rely on contributions from the public. Were it not for my constitutional rights, which they have helped preserve, I would not live in a free and democratic country where one can still speak his mind, within reason of course.

First Amendment to the U.S. Constitution:

"Congress shall make no law respecting an establishment of religion, or prohibiting the free exercise thereof, or abridging the freedom of speech, or of the press: or the right of the people peaceably to assemble and to petition the Government for a redress of grievances."

Regretfully, the great U.S. Constitution, which separated powers in order that there be a fair system of checks and balances, will be circumvented by the globalists in the future via a massive campaign which will be sold to the people as being in "everyone's best interests," hence, a New World Order.

While some theologians have delved into the ethical messages of the scriptures and concluded they are absolutely liberal, which is just as wrong as claiming they are absolutely conservative, I intend to prove they are a unique blend of both. Because I am on the defensive, for the sake of the common person, this writing warrants a slight incline toward the liberal, as this is often where true righteousness lies in this politically conservative and judgmental world. Since true righteousness flows from a spirit of brotherly love, it is often easier for the modest liberal to fully grasp the essence of what the "11th commandment" (to love one another) means – John 13:34-35. Liberalism is as old as humankind and has been under steady attack from the Far- Right for at least the last two decades. It is a "threatened species" of sorts which has been declared "evil" by many within the Far-Right. As revived during the seventeenth and eighteenth centuries to some degree, it became clear that it would ultimately be a philosophy which the rightist-Church would have to reckon with and eventually incorporate in order to keep it from becoming totally autonomous.

Today, the term liberal has been tossed around by many conservatives to describe sinful and ungodly ideology. A liberal is now classified as being reprehensible and loathsome, to say the least. Since the liberal is often deemed a "leftist," some (ie: The "Una-bomber") make such ridiculous and unfounded claims that leftists suffer from low self-esteem, self-hatred, inferiority complexes, and depressive tendencies. People of all walks of life are affected by the above, including right-wingers (note: a lack of self-esteem and self-hatred is oftentimes correlated to right-wing racism). Additionally, the self-righteous Far-Right is self-absorbed and haughty, thus, not level headed, down to earth, humane, kind, gentle, compassionate, merciful, or just – as Christ was. Thus, Far-Right conservatives are anti-Christ.

Many hardened conservatives make a mockery out of "the liberal animal-rights groups," for instance, as though they were doing wrong. Some even claim that an animal does not have a spirit, therefore, science should have carte blanche to experiment as they want. Scientists should be able to experiment on some animals (ie: pigs, rodents), while adhering to a professional code of conduct. I also do not believe it was God's intention that men imprison animals in cages or mammals in aquariums for their profit as do many in the "animal entertainment business." Ecclesiastes 3:21 clearly reveals that animals do have a spirit. This should not be a point for "over-compensating." There have been legal motions which actually go too far in protecting some animals. I am not suggesting that some should not be eaten, either (see Leviticus 11). I am simply protesting much of the Far-Right's animal abuses and experimentation over the last 75 years or so – not to mention biological and scientific experiments actually conducted on humans. Surely, Jesus loved animals — though his diet was not à la Vaticana.

Mockery is made of the generosity of the liberal as though this were wrong. 2 Corinthians 9:6 clearly explains the universal law that one will be compensated according to how one sows, sparingly or bountifully, liberally or conservatively. To be liberal means to be: generous, considerate, not strict or rigid, open minded, gentle, and tolerant – among others, like kind-hearted. All of these and many more apply beautifully to Christ if one truly looks deeply into his personality. On the other hand, conservative frequently means to be: stingy, inconsiderate, strict and rigid, narrow-minded, harsh, intolerant, and tending to preserve, or as this book will show, revive established institutions. It is a fact that those who were "closed-minded" or overly conservative were in fact among those who needed their minds opened to the scriptures in Luke 24:45. It is precisely the intolerance of the hardened right-wing, high-caliber Catholic clergy who have not seen that their "zero tolerance" over the centuries has been the very root of the Church's horrors toward other peoples.

Though it is the Far-Right which deserves a negative image, it is now the liberal who is associated with the ugly deeds of man's past. A twisted interpretation is at issue here in that the liberal-minded are typecast as wonton, wild, weak, and wicked when this is the furthest from the truth. A righteous liberal is sensible, strong, self- restrained, and spiritual. The modest liberal, who is now virtually despised, is primarily who I give credit to because "the leftist" has often fought for the principles which Christ himself stood for. Yet this world, being quite conservative through the ages, has turned everything "upside down" and made wrong much of what is right. The modest liberal should not be associated with the extremes of the squalid Sodomites, as their lifestyle reflected a lewd, licentious, and lawless culture, none of which are synonyms of liberal. To those of an extreme rightist, anti-liberal mindset, it may come as a shock that there are a considerable amount of Biblical authors who were not necessarily of the conservative nest. Proverbs 11:25 portrays a "liberal man" in a very positive light, in a manner consistent with the blessings of the "laws of retribution" which are common to most religions around the world. Moreover, the description in Micah 7:18-20 of God is indicative of a partly "liberal God" (not to be taken out of context), one who is truly forgiving, merciful, compassionate, and loving. This perfectly balanced God with a variety of liberal or leftist ethics is profoundly opposed to the parallel "politically correct" dynamics between today's superficially "inclusive-Church" and the "inclusive-Right."

Since the right-wing has incorporated a strictly conservative interpretation of the scriptures into the political and cultural arenas as being politically, morally, and ethically correct, the masses are subjected to a biased viewpoint. Many Protestants and traditionalists who are led astray by this deceived perception of just who Christ really was are being blinded by the "Luciferian light" of this apostate new age and its many conservative false prophets claiming to be apostles of Christ. This is not to say that false prophets solely arise from the Far-Right. However, the fundamentalist position of many can only be born of this sort of ideology. Also, the vast majority of mainstream Christian teachers, preachers, evangelists, revivalists, reverends, and pastors – having more conservative overtones – make the math quite elementary.

Without a doubt, the most perplexing of all conflicts within the dynamics of the Church has been, "Why doesn't the doctrine of the geo-political Catholic Church, The Holy Bible, which ironically they helped bring to the world, provide a source of reference for so many of its basic beliefs?" This question really encompasses a series of very conflicting and thought-provoking issues, which although not new, being of the conservative traditional faith (and in some cases meshed into government), need to be re-addressed to some degree and viewed in a new light. Making clear distinctions regarding the Church's conflicts with The Bible will serve to better understand the intricacies of some prophecies as they relate to modern day political developments which will culminate into the final "Egypt" (explained in the latter part of this writing).

Among some of the most obvious ones, are: The universal Roman-Gregorian time-clock and calendar, Sunday, Christmas, New Year, Valentines Day, Easter, idol worship, the state of the dead, purgatory, baptism, and Christ's physical traits / the "race card."

GOD'S HOLY DAYS / ROME'S HOLIDAYS
I would like to initially make two high points quite clear: {1} the fact that from the very first week of recorded time in the book of Genesis, when God finished his creations, He and those with him, aka: Elohim, rested on the seventh day (Genesis 2:2-3). Granted, it may be that this "week" was actually seven years, not seven days. Regardless, this fact greatly supports the time-clock of the ancient Hebrews as being "at one" with the One True God. These days were divided into half light and half dark which indicates that the very beginning of our universe was itself equally balanced. {2}It is essential for Christians to remember that our Messiah, Jesus Christ, Mary his mother, and every one of his disciples – being true Jews – observed the Hebrew time-clock. This included the Sabbath and the Hebrew Holy Days spelled out in Leviticus 23 and continued in The New Testament – basically the opposite of Rome's time-clock and holidays (Matthew 26:17-19; Mark 1:21).

~ TIME ~
Time is a wonder,
It has no beginning, it has no end,
Always continues
Like day, like night,
Time comes and goes
Not revealing its course,
Leaving us only the past,
God-like, in that Time
You can't touch

L.F.G.

SUNDAY, DAY OF THE SUN

Since the number seven (among others) has such profound Mosaic / prophetic mystery attached to it, as we see throughout both testaments, it makes perfect sense that there is an unexplained reason why God explicitly picked the seventh day, not the first day of the week, to be reserved for him. Joshua 6:4, *"And seven priests shall bear seven trumpets of rams' horns before the ark and on the seventh day you shall march around the city seven times, the priests blowing their trumpets."* Leviticus 25:8, *"And you shall count seven weeks of years, seven times seven years, so that the time of the seven weeks of years shall be to you forty nine years."* Known as the "passion sayings," for instance, Christ's last [seven] words fall right in place with all other numeric mysteries. Zechariah 4:10 speaks of God's [seven] eyes, while Revelations 4:5 reveals his [seven] spirits. There are numerous other examples in the Bible which correlate the number seven to the heavens, for it is there that the mysteries behind these apparent "quirks" are known.

Sunday, the first day of the week under our Roman time-clock, is the ancient Babylonian day set aside from the other six days of the week to honor Sun-Ra/Re, or the solar deity. In ancient times, nations gave heed to sun worship. Virtually every culture had some form of sun worship meshed into its fabric of life, from Sunna -the Teutonic and Scandinavian Sun Goddess to the Dawn Goddess, Usha, of India to the Hsi Wang Mu Goddess of China to the Greek Sun God Helios to the Amaterasu Sun Goddess of Japan to the Persian Sun God, Mithras. Rome, in following these footsteps, took on the honoring of the sun and called it Sol-Invictus, hence, why so many countries keep Sunday sacred today. Emperor Constantine then adopted and consecrated this day as the official day of rest for the Roman Empire. As time passed, Rome incorporated this belief into its ideology, giving homage to the venerable day of the sun. Specifically, it was Constantine who officially instituted this day as the day of rest for the Empire.

From before the founding of the United States we have seen the almighty hand of Rome intertwined into our partly Protestant culture via its Sunday Blue Laws. These were laws which were implemented by the U.S. government to ordain this 1st day of the week (see any Roman calendar) as the day of rest. There are some cases on record which reveal just how much Rome's Sunday cult has been woven into our culture. Despite the dormant state of these laws, many states still adhere to them, through, for instance, their established Sunday liquor restrictions. So we see, that sun-worship has been passed down through time by these ancient civilizations to this very day, and, without a doubt, it is directly linked to rightist-Rome. It is in concordance that since Lucifer was the "light- bearer" in the heavens, he would use the "light" of this world as a means of diverting the fidelity of man away from the one true God.

In recent times, we have been acclimated to the honor of the sun-god subliminally in our music, as in, "Open up your heart and let the sun shine in" or "Aquarius – Let the sun shine" as examples. On a popular Sunday morning show, it is the sun which is imbedded into the program – not to mention the eye-ball insignia which some corporations also use (more on this in chapter eight).

Another angle from which to see this overall picture of the replacement of Sunday over the true Saturday Sabbath, the one which the Son followed being a Jew, is that the name itself invokes the concept of it being the "son's day" or "son-day" – as in Christ the Son. Though the Son was a Sabbatarian, many ultra-conservative folk get tied up in the legalism surrounding the fourth commandment, thus, becoming as many of the Scribes and Pharisees in their dialogues with Christ over the law. Christ did indeed keep this seventh day as holy – that is a fact.

However, since his righteousness is so far above that of man, many then as today, miss the weightier matters which allow for some leeway regarding what one should do on this day as is shown throughout the New Testament. Though there is no question as to when the Sabbath day actually is, nowhere in the Bible does it state explicitly how one is to keep it holy. Some balance is very crucial or one may end up looking like the fools who pointed fingers and threw their nets to try to catch Christ in a conflict of law to no avail. (Exodus 20:8-11; Deuteronomy 17:3; Luke 4:16; Luke 6; Luke 13:10-17; Luke 14:1-6; Hebrews 4:3-13)

CHRISTMAS

At the risk of sounding like the "grinch" to some, I will delve into this holiday, not holy-day. Christmas actually originated in Egypt and was later incorporated into Rome's festivals. In the days of old, as the change of seasons came, certain festivities became customary among many people around the world. Winter solstice, for instance, was actually the festival many people celebrated on or around December 25th – nowhere in the Bible is this day proclaimed, nor did Christ ever instruct his followers to celebrate the day he entered this world – fittingly, his true date of birth is a mystery, as is the date of his return.

Interesting to note that it was a decrease in sunlight which was at the root of this holiday. Surely, those cults who thought that God was the sun and the sun was God, were in essence praying that the sun come again soon. We must keep in mind that many people were (and are to this day) very superstitious, as was for example, the notion that light / day was perceived as good while darkness / night was interpreted as evil. This belief is quite wrong, for it is God who creates darkness as well as light – Isaiah 45:7. Among the people who celebrated this change of season were, for instance, the people of Iran with their observance of Yalda or the Chineese Dong Zhi – "the arrival of winter." But only Rome overlaid this winter solstice with the birth of the Messiah. Rome integrated these customs with the birth of Christ and gave us the holiday we all know as Christmas. For multiple reasons, Satan and his disciples use the holiday season to their advantage. The manipulation of mankind's disposition is one of great interest to the evil empire, as depression and "the blues" set in particularly strong for some during the holidays. The lack of sunlight coupled with the financial burdens brought by these weeks of consumerism are factors which the globalists find much too pleasurable to overlook as a perfect timeframe to get people into debt while they pocket big money.

Incidentally, Santa Claus may very well be the most diabolical / anti-Christ mythical figure to come out of any pagan holiday, as it is he who brings gifts and happiness to children, not Christ. Is it just another coincidence that Satan and Santa have the same letters and sound so alike? Lets examine this a bit more. Another name for God is "El Shaddai." In contrast to El (Latin for him) and in conjunction with the universal negative, no, we get No-El / Noel. As Christ, Santa is portrayed as one who comes swiftly to judge those who have done good and bad, as a timeless icon who has authority to bring compensation / reward to those who have done good. It is certainly worth noting that Christ is described as a man having "hair as white wool" – Rev 1:14.

As to the Christmas tree: *"Hear the word which the Lord speaks to you, O house of Israel. Thus says the Lord: Learn not the way of the nations, nor be dismayed at the signs of the heavens because the nations are dismayed at them, for the customs of the people's are false. A tree from the forest is cut down, and worked with an axe by the hands of a craftsman. Men deck it with gold and silver ; they fasten it with hammer and nails so that it cannot move. Their idols are like scarecrows in a cumber field...."* (Jeremiah 10:1-5). Many "Protestant" churches continue the Christmas tradition with all of its customs even though it is a holiday with no Biblical reference whatsoever. It is odd that so many Protestant congregations protest part of the Vatican's dogma, yet integrate many of Rome's holidays into their church services. This is not only the case in America, but throughout the world. (Note: the U.N. also honors this holiday; Luard, pp.40-50).

Though, Christmas is very much a man-made holiday which is without question the most un-Christian commercialized and materialistic of all holidays, thus, not among the Biblical holy-days, we must not discard the depth of Christ's weightier messages. Therefore, if one were to do good for his family, for widows, for children, or for his fellow man during the festivities of Christmas, that would be synonymous with the pure essence of Christ's parables which gave priority to the weightier matters of this life.

NEW YEAR

New Year, or December 31st, which globally marks the dawn of a new Roman year is another mark of the Gregorian time-clock. Jews who wish others a "happy new year" on this day do not dilute their spirituality in the least; likewise, true Christians should do the same. Will it hurt Christians to respect Jews who do not adhere to Rome's festivals and maybe even wish them a "happy new year" when their new year roles around? One can separate from the customs of "the nations" as mentioned above, yet be courteous and warm to others.

EASTER

This is another holiday which Rome incorporated into its festivals. It really gives homage to Ishtar, the Babylonian goddess of fertility (which is why the Easter bunny- rabbit lays eggs). Passover, which is among the Biblical holy days was replaced by Rome long ago in an effort to detour as many as possible from the truth. Jesus Christ and his disciples kept these holy days as is clear in Matthew 26:18, *"He said, Go into the city to a certain one, and say to him, The teacher says, My time is at hand; I will keep the Passover at your house with my disciples."* In short, the bunny rabbit and Santa Clause are both prodigies of meticulous wizardry. There is no mention in the Bible as to Easter.

DAY OF "LOVE" (VALENTINE'S DAY / "LUPERCALIA")

Since romance is a beautiful part of mankind, would Satan have a reason to "put in his two cents" on the matter? As is no shock, he has used Rome to continue the indirect worship of the "Greek gods/goddesses" (ie: Venus, Eros/Cupid, Ahprodite). It is peculiar that "Roma" is "Amor" (love) spelled backwards, or in other words, "flip-flopped." As with other holidays, there is a commercial / profit factor for the globalists.

IDOL WORSHIP

The worship of idols is a most critical issue which so many seem to overlook to this day. To God Almighty, it takes such priority as to be the essential topic of the first and second commandments of Exodus 20. Only **Yahweh-God** is to be "worshipped." It is clear that this particular sin has always been the most offensive of any sin mankind could commit under the sun during his brief visit to this planet. It is crucial then, to fully understand the weight this carries, as it comprises a variety of ways in which man falls by the wayside into condemnation. This is often done through ignorance and a lack of desire to question tradition and why one is venerating or bowing to any other god, including goddesses, angels, saints, images, or fellow human beings. Even John, to whom the book of Revelations is credited, was unclear as to this most delicate issue of "worship." Revelations 22:8-9: *"...I fell down to worship at the feet of the angel...but he said to me, You must not do that!"*

At the risk of coming across as a devil to some, I am compelled to focus on Mary, Mother of Jesus. Certainly, Mary was of the finest class of women, pristine in character and dignity, of utmost moral fiber and graciousness. As Sarah, Manoah's wife, and Elizabeth, Mother of John the Baptist, she was "visited" (ie: impregnated) by an angel of God, chosen among women to serve the heavens. For them, as for anyone else who serves God, this was not only an honor of the highest degree, but a blessing for mankind (Genesis 18 and Judges 13). Among the many idols one finds in the Church, Mary is the most revered. Sacred to many as Christ himself, the worship of Mary has been like that of ancient goddesses – ie: Athena, the Greek Goddess or Shiva Ardanari, an Indian half- woman Lord. However, nowhere in the Bible is there even one reference which remotely gives credence to praying to her or venerating her. Not once did Christ mention his earthly mother as one to be given homage to as one would the celestial Father.

In chapter two we will read more on the power of Mary and today's cultural parallels to the Babylonian goddesses of yesterday. Needless to say, if this is the case with Mary, neither should we venerate the saints, for they were also mortals who passed away and are awaiting the final judgement day like everyone else (second commandment – Exodus 20:4-6). Deuteronomy 27:15: *"Cursed be the man who makes a graven image or molten image, an abomination to the Lord, a thing made by the hands of a craftsman..."*

THE STATE OF THE DEAD AND PURGATORY
Though there is absolutely nothing wrong with honoring someone who has died, there is a problem when that honor turns to worship.

One of the most essential beliefs of the Catholic doctrine has been that of teaching its adherents that the spirit of man enters a third dimension and thus is not "asleep" as the Bible claims. The concept of being able to work out one's salvation after death is not new at all. It is reminiscent of eastern philosophy (ie: reincarnation) in that through a payment for the "bad karma" one has accumulated, there is a spiritual sort of amnesty which takes effect. The penitence ordered by a Catholic priest after one confesses his or her bad deeds is "right up this alley" as well. Therefore, a couple aspects of eastern religions are also woven into Catholicism.

Throughout the Bible there are clear and convincing excerpts which support the belief that upon death, one enters a state of rest/ sleep while awaiting the final trumpet to sound off prior to the day of judgement. Absolutely nowhere in the Bible is there any excerpt that could be even remotely interpreted as being of or synonymous to purgatory – the notion of a temporary spiritual pit-stop to pay for one's bad deeds until getting the green light to move on to heaven. Mankind, upon death, is in a state of sleep awaiting the "last trumpet" to sound off (just as we are awakened in this life by an alarm clock) – then we will all be judged at the final judgement. If there was any mention of this pre-celestial pit-stop in the scriptures, it would be in direct conflict with the following Biblical excerpts: Deuteronomy 31:16; 1 Kings 14:31; Ecclesiastes 9:4-10; Isaiah 26:19; John 3:13; 1 Corinthians 15:51-53; 1 Thessalonians 4:16-18; Revelation 20:12-15.

NECROMANCY

The "science" of necromancy further proves the fundamental wickedness which is indeed inherent in the belief that the dead are roaming around in a third dimension. Necromancy, which has deep roots in ancient diabolic doctrines (ie: The Book of the Dead / Egypt) was thoroughly denounced by God in the Old Testament as a result of many Jews who swayed toward ancient Jewish mysticism. *Deuteronomy 18: 9-12, "When you come into the land which the Lord your God gives you, you shall not learn to follow the abominable practices of those nations. There shall not be found among you anyone who burns his son or his daughter as an offering, anyone who practices divination, a soothsayer, or an augur, or a sorcerer, or a charmer, or a medium, or a wizard or a necromancer. For whoever does these things is an abomination to the Lord; and because of these abominable practices the Lord your God is driving them out before you."*

BAPTISM

The Catholic method of enacting this ceremony, as many know, is by sprinkling holy water on the infant baby's forehead. The theme throughout the New Testament is that if one is not baptized, as John baptized Jesus – by submergence, one cannot enter the kingdom of God. Though this exclusionary position is somewhat questionable on the surface, as there is no mention of this in the Old Testament, one might be more apt to repent of one's sins and be baptized by submergence anyway – as the cliche says, "better safe than sorry" (Matthew 3:16). According to the scriptures, repentance and baptism can lead one "out of Egypt" and into the kingdom.

ISRAELITES, CHRIST, AND "THE RACE CARD"

The following is also in honor of those who like Lyndon B. Johnson and Dr. Martin Luther King, are pro-civil rights, thus, against the racist machine which was so prevalent just a few decades ago:

Due to the overwhelming influence of Hollywood and the media, I am not surprised by the false notion of so many people regarding the term Jew. Many believe Jews are solely the European Jews who dominate today's Israel. Fact is, there have always been many Jews – African, Arabic, Oriental, etc. At present time, modern science is investigating the claim of some black Jews, among them, the Lemba who have been put under the microscope through DNA testing (and what is known as the "Cohen / Cohanin -Y- Chromosome Analysis") and proven to have similar genetic make-up as that of Old Testament Semitic peoples. The Lemba assert that they are among the "lost tribes" of the house of Israel, as they adhere to the Old Testament dietary and cultural statutes. Could some of those who claim to be "Israelites" today actually be impersonators? How many others around the world have ties to the lost tribes and do not know it? In John 10:16 Christ proclaimed, *"I have other sheep which are not of this fold."* In Luke 7:9, Christ said, *"I tell you not even in Israel have I found such faith."* Christ does not see mankind by race, as "majority" or "minority" – as black or white, as Asian or Hispanic. He sees us as beings of the human race with no distinction between one or the other, for all fall short of being pure, perfect, or sinless. Though *"the Jews are entrusted with the oracles of God"* (Romans 3:2), the fact is Galatians 3:28 sums it up well: *"There is neither Jew nor Greek, there is neither slave nor free, there is neither male nor female; for you are all one in Christ."* The Apostle Paul also acknowledged that he was *"an Israelite"* (Romans 11:1). Through faith in Jesus Christ and truly following his footsteps one becomes an Israelite irrelevant of origin or race. See Matthew 15:21-28 and Hebrews 11.

Christ himself has been re-invented in more ways than simply being illustrated as a conservative, which although forgiving and generous, he is still portrayed as very much a white right-winger at heart. His conservative side has been unduly amplified to suit the hierarchical authorities in their domination over the masses and subsequent oppression of those who we in America consider minorities. At the forefront of the various myths taught by the racist-Church, lies the mistaken perception that he was a fair-skinned Messiah. Though ultimately it really does not matter if he was or was not, I will delve into this for the sake of the debate, as it is important to many people.

In the New Testament it refers to the Messiah-Christ as being of the genealogy of the Hebrew King David, Father of Solomon. These Old Testament characters are among those who have been portrayed as white men by the white establishment of which Hollywood has magnified that perception. All three were most likely of a darker skin tone as that of the Arab people of the regions of Palestine. Here in the west one may refer to this complexion as dark-tanned or brown. If Christ's skin tone was that of a northerner (European), would he have not stuck out like a sore thumb in that region of the world 2000 years ago? Herod's orders would have most likely been, "Go kill all white baby boys under two years of age" -not- "Go kill all baby boys under two years of age." It would be much more feasible to conclude that Christ was not white as depicted by the Vatican. As will be revealed in later chapters, the fact that "the middle ground" is where God is in various respects, it also makes sense that from a strictly racial perspective, Christ was somewhere between black and white. He came from the genetic lineage of Solomon (certainly not a name associated with the white race; neither are Isaiah, Zechariah, Zephaniah, Nehemiah, Jeremiah, Ezekiel, Joshua). Christ could not have been the white Messiah which Rome invented for a few reasons. See Song of Solomon.

Michael Angelo, Rembrant, Leonardo da Vincci, and the rest of the Romanesque artists were under the direction of their superiors to create the universal illusion of a "white-only" heaven as seen in all of their works throughout every cathedral in Italy and throughout the world. Their very famous works of art, beautiful as they were (though they would be more beautiful if they were not white-only), were inclined solely toward the aesthetic eye of one audience while demeaning the rights of passage into heaven for anyone of any color. In an effort to make him a feasible savior to the European peoples in particular, Christ's whole persona was altered to create a more perfect union with what might be expected of the Messiah in that region of the world – western Europe. This massive change was the result of clever and calculated moves to solidify the white- authority to one major power-house which would prove to be the very source which God would ironically use to "spread the word" to the four corners of the planet: Rome. It is not surprising that a recent report by National Geographic titled "Inside the Vatican" revealed the fact that only Swiss males are allowed to become bodyguards for the pope to this day. It should also be noted that the "halo" which was placed around the heads of Christ, Mary, and the saints was the result of overlapping the sun deity with the Messiah and others. This alone should raise a red flag for those who fail to see that Rome imbedded ancient paganism even into the imagery of their brand of Christianity.

I truly salute many Caucasians in the last two centuries (and those of like-mind throughout time), mostly democrats in this country, who have risen above the racism to a higher level of consciousness which is about as close to true righteousness as we will see in this world. What this country would be like now had they not fought for justice and liberty would be reminiscent of the backward ways of yesterday. It is they who deserve applause for going against the wicked trends of the Far-Right, for they did not adhere to the establishment and objectives of the conservative-racist-machine. To those who have sacrificed a great deal in going against the flow, in being insulted oftentimes by their own families, in showing their true colors, God will recompense greatly in accordance with his universal laws of retribution.

Affirmative action, which was an attempt at balancing the scales of the right-wing's racist regime, was the product of a higher conscience among some fine white democrats who truly upheld Biblical doctrine. Abolishing it was wrong. It is certainly not that minorities have reached equilibrium in the business world, as it would take numerous decades of affirmative action to really undo the damage which was caused by the Far- Right over the last few centuries. It is reprehensible that here we are in the year 2002 and instead of progressing, we are actually regressing to the discriminatory days of yesterday as a result of today's "upside down" reasoning. This is sold to the masses as righteous, yet has hidden agendas and detrimental consequences for minorities. In the foreground, this wickedness is covered by "fairness issues" while in the background lies the truth which is rightist racism in all facets of life. This is initiating a "politically correct" brand of Jim Crow. Regretfully, the twisted logic of today is taking us back to yesterday, except for now it is under the banner of "it's for the good of minorities."

Racial profiling, which also was sold under positive pretenses, has done more harm than good, as it was among the seeds that the globalists planted some years ago in our legal system to escalate inner conflict and racially divide the U.S. even more. It is interesting that following the Oklahoma City bombing by Timothy McVeigh, Caucasians were certainly not scrutinized as others are now. Caucasians have not been subjected to great scrutiny within the school system, either, despite the fact that, most, if not all, terrorist activity in America's schools has been inflicted by middle-class non-Hispanic white males.

In retrospect, those on the other end of the spectrum (the hardened right), God will condemn and curse for their gross insensitivity and inhumanity. Hatred and hate- crimes are as demons to mankind, as plagues to the land, as curses to society. Though there are good and bad men of all races, as there are bigots of all colors, there has been an overwhelming amount of hatred from many whites toward blacks, non-white Hispanics, Arabs, Asians, Indians, etc. Fact is, whites cannot disagree that they have more racist- based and hatred-filled organizations than any other race on earth. No other race seems to hate so deeply, so fervently, to the point of hanging a man from a tree, literally burning a man at the stake, tearing his intestines to shreds, or dragging him from the back of a truck until he dies just because he is not white. The irony is that if any have a reason to hate, it is those who have been terrorized by being deemed inferior, enslaved, raped, pillaged, plundered, tortured, robbed, beaten, and degraded to the level of an animal – or lower. Consequently, if a white racist points a finger at a yellow, red, brown, or black racist saying "you are as guilty of being a bigot as I am"- I would have to disagree.

Reverse racism, however, is still racism, no matter how one paints the picture. Two wrongs don't make a right. To the racist blacks, I ask, how are you rising above the wickedness of the racism of some white men when you are returning the same brand of hatred to all whites? For that matter, even if you return that hatred only to the white racists, is that elevating you over their lowly selves even in the least? Some blacks have taken an over-compensatory position against whites, so much so as to severely err in claiming that all whites are racist evil pigs or that Christianity is the "white man's" religion. Again, true Christianity is not race based. Then there are the blacks who are overly sensitive, concluding that however whites refer to blacks, even with tact, it is somehow racist. Regretfully, Christianity has been ruled by Rome. Thus, it has been interpreted as belonging to and originating from "the white man." This could not be further from the truth. This false and misleading conclusion has caused many blacks to feel like outcasts with no sense of belonging, thus, many are turning to non-Christian beliefs. The magnitude of this concept is multiplied by the considerable lack of education common among blacks and the fact that they, having been stripped of their roots, have relatively no ties to their African kinfolk. Some feel they have been excluded from a white-only heaven. This is precisely what some racists propose, ascertaining that blacks were cursed through Ham (Genesis 9:1 proves otherwise; 1 Corinthians 12-13 sums this issue up quite well).

The Far-Right is indeed where racism is primarily found; and to be racist is synonymous with evil. One finds that all-too-frequently the term "nigger" is used by racists. Little do they know that it may be they who are the niggers, for this is not a term which defines color of skin, but color of character and color of integrity. Hence, there are niggers of all classes and all races.

Many Hispanic illegal immigrants, too, are classified as "cockroaches" and thoroughly degraded as though they were less-than-human. While the Far-Right claims that these groups are taking jobs from Americans, there are few, if any, Americans willing to do the work which these modern day slaves do for the minimal wages they are paid. What our grocery bill would be without them is something to think about. Woe to those who abuse of the hired hand! America is presently what it is, the world's superpower, because of the unique blend of all immigrants. Americans should never lose sight of the poem by Emma Lazarus which appears at the base of the Statue of Liberty: *"Give me your tired, your poor, your huddled masses yearning to breathe free..."* This obviously includes people of all races. I realize there must be limitations to "open borders," but for those who come here to do hard labor which directly impacts the economy for the better, a new attitude toward the hired hand is long over due.

To be engulfed with rightist racism as is the European Freedom Party, KKK, Nazi, Skinhead, Superior White Power Militants (SWP's), White /Aryan Supremist Movements, the now "inclusive" Vatican, many republicans, and even some democrats is to show that one's spirit is tainted with the venom of the snake (Satan). Those who proclaim an affinity to the Democratic Party, but are inwardly racist, ravenous wolves are actually more of a threat to minorities than those of the Far-Right who are clearly identified as "the enemy." This brand of democrat is very much a serpent in disguise, a demon dressed as an angel. It could actually be said, that a black, brown, yellow, or red person who has disowned their own and serves to further suppress their people by playing into or joining forces with the Far-Right is the truest form of a "cockroach" – ironic as it may sound from one who is defending minorities. This, by the way, is as gross and exceedingly powerful a mechanism of the Far-Right as any of the right-wing conspiracies which are present even within the left: the Far-Right will make "sell outs" out of some among the left. Thus, it is clear and convincing evidence that the Far-Right has such a long-arm as to penetrate even the opposition.

This Far-Right has historically been the aggressor as was quite clear during the inquisitions. Only a predominantly pro-rightist mandate would be capable of force- feeding the savior to the west as was the case during 'The Inquisition' of the Americas by rightist-Rome. Most, if not all, of the superiors of the missionaries who brought Christ to this hemisphere were certainly not liberal-minded. They were harsh, brutal, closed-minded, intolerant, cold, and hard-hearted. Regrettably, in order to seed the planet with the good news of Christ, the Church did feed the native Indian peoples of our hemisphere, not to mention other peoples of the world (ie: Australian Aborigines), in a very un-Christ-like fashion – in a very ultra-right, self-righteous, and reprehensible manner. To suggest that God would approve of this cold and callous treatment of others, their land, rights, and possessions to save the masses from being sent to hell would be hypocritical at best.

Only God knows why he allows what seems inconceivable to human logic to occur and even worse, to reoccur, so it is not for mankind to decipher why he would allow such apparent travesties of justice to take place. Moreover, for these events to happen in the name of Christ is that much more mind-boggling. Thus, to dwell on why this all took place the way it did would be not only beyond us to reason, but it would border on insanity. No one, except perhaps the hard-right within the Church and their racist allies, could argue that the manner in which the Church made "disciples of all nations" is not at all consistent with the mission given in Matthew 28:19-20.

Furthermore, if the people who were to be baptized and made disciples did not want to be baptized or become disciples, the Church missionaries were never instructed to persecute them but to "move on" (Luke 9:5). It is clear why the Church may be reluctant to take a close look into the past, for it is there that much of "the blood of the saints" was spilled. Yes, the Church has apologized to some extent, and we are to forgive and let God take his revenge out on those who have done evil when he is ready. But we cannot forget these atrocities and these blatantly hardened rightist (not righteous) acts in the name of God, as there are lessons to learn and corrections to make also "in the name of God." Sometimes too, an apology which is seemingly sincere, but is in reality merely superficial, is like putting a band-aid on a broken leg.

SELECTED CREDITS

Comay & Brownrigg, *"Who's Who in the Bible."* New York, NY: Wing Books,1971.

Jobe Martin, D.M.D., *"The Evolution of a Creationist."* Rockwall, Texas: Biblical Discipleship Publishers, 1994. {The Ten Commandments, Ch 6}

Turn Left: *"Accomplishments of Liberalism"* (www.cjnetworks.com/~cubsfan/libgood.html)

Paralyzed Veterans of America (www.pva.org)

The United States Constitution, Collier's Encyclopedia Vol.7. Great Britain: The Crowell-Collier Publishing Co.,1963. {Separation of Powers}

Una-Bomber's Full Text Manifesto, pp 2-3.

The Tampa Tribune, Howard Troxler, *"Plight of Pigs in the Family Way Points to Weighty Idea,"* January 18, 2002. {"Overcompensation" of animal rights}

El Tiempo, Luis Carlos Gomez Diaz, *"Corte / Debate sobre descanso y libertad religiosa"* / *"Court / Debate as to day of rest and religious liberty,"* Bogota, Colombia, Mayo 5, 2000 / May 5, 2000.

Shabat, Sensacion Inexplicable / Sabbath, Inexplicable Sensation. www.hebreos.net/Judaismo/shabsi.html Pope

John Paul, *"Dies Domini,"* May 31, 1998.

Catechism of the Catholic Church, Vatican City, 1994.

Catholic Encyclopedia: *Dies Solis / Sunday*

Encyclopedia Britannica (11ᵗʰ ed.) art. *Sunday*

Chamber's Encyclopedia / Constantine / (1882 ed.) Vol. VIII, p. 401, art. *Sabbath*

Carlyle B. Haynes, *"From Sabbath To Sunday."* Hagerstown, Md: Review & Herald Publishing Association, 1928. {Change of Sabbath and Calendar}

The Washington Post, Bill Broadway, *"When is the Lord's Day?"* January 23,1999.

Wayne Muller, *"Sabbath: Restoring the Sacred Rhythm of Rest."* New York: Bantam Books,1999.

Pamela R. Tepper, *"The Law of Contracts and the Uniform Commercial Code."* Albany, New York: West Publishing,1995.{Sunday Laws, P.107}

U.S. Government Printing Office via GPO Access, *"McGowan V. Maryland,"* Case # 366US420, May 29, 1961 – 220 MD. 117,151 A.2D 156, Affirmed.

Sun Gods: www.paganquest.com

Notes on Sol Invictus: www.novaroma.org

Evan Luard, *"The United Nations: How it Works and What it does."* New York: St. Martin's Press, 1994.{Christmas}

Calendars and their History, Explanatory Supplement to the Astronomical Almanac.

The New York Times, Alessandra Stanley, *"Pope Offers Way Out of Purgatory for Deeds During Millenium,"* 1999.

NOVA, *"Cohanin Analysis"*: The Lemba, 2000.

The Discovery Channel, *"Jesus: The Complete Story,"* April 2001. {What Did He Look Like?}

The Tampa Tribune – Faith & Values, *"A New Look at Jesus,"* April 14, 2001. {What Did He Look Like?}

National Geographic, *"Inside the Vatican,"* 2001.{Only Swiss Bodyguards}

Time Magazine, Nancy Gibbs, *"Botching the Big Case: The People v. Timothy McVeigh – Could it have been a wider conspiracy?"* May 21, 2001.

The New York Times, Alessandra Stanley, *"Vatican Examines Role of Church in Inquisition,"* Sunday, November 1, 1998. {Spanish Inquisition}

The New Book of Knowledge, *Aborigines*, Vol. I, Danbury, Connecticut: Grolier, 2001.

Ken Blady, *"Jewish Communities in Exotic Places."* Northvale, NJ: Jason Aranson Inc., 2000.

International Herald Tribune, Alessandra Stanley for NY Times Service, *"Vatican*

to Apologize within Limits," Paris, France, March 2, 2000. {The Holocaust}
Time Magazine, David Van Biema / New York, *"Loose Lips Sink Fellowships,"*
August 6, 2001. {Pope Pius XII's role in World War II}
El Tiempo, Olga Lucia Lozano y Juanita Leon, *"Los 7 pecados capitales de la
Iglesia"* – *"The 7 capital sins of the Church"* – Bogota, Colombia; Domingo
28 de Febrero de 1999 / Sunday 28th of February,1999. {Abuso de Los
Indigenas / Abuse of The Indigenous Peoples}

CHAPTER TWO

THE EXTREME LEFT

Culture changes during the 1960s opened a plethora of extremist movements which have taken their toll on society and the family unit very much for the negative. As a driver of a car "over-compensates" to avoid an accident where one or two may die, yet ends up killing three or four, so is the case with extreme-leftist groups that have brought their abominable ideals to the forefront in the last few decades as though they were "all good." Prior to delving into the other extreme, a peculiar phenomenon is oftentimes a reality (which will be interwoven into other issues throughout this book): the ever-so-hypocritical Far-Right not only engages in many of the very acts they condemn, but entraps, exploits, and profits from the extreme leftists in their folly. In order to claim heroic deeds to the public at large, the Far-Right then establishes a "moral war" opposing the very debauchery they helped fuel – how Luciferic of them!

RADICAL FEMINISM
With good reason and perhaps well-intended, the feminist-movement attempted to undo the wrongs inflicted by the unjust Far-Right for so long. Extremists like the Taliban who's interpretation of the Koran severely warps any potential for women to exercise their rights are not so different from the hard right hand of Rome in ages past. It is a severe travesty that in this modern day, girls and women around the world continue to be treated as dogs, used as prostitutes, and exchanged like cattle by men who have only profit in mind. There are

thousands suffering as literal slaves of "organizations" which are run by men who are "cockroaches." Some cultures throughout the world allow for mutilation and degradation of girls and women which to our western minds is inconceivable. The U.N., which has some good intentions, is trying to tackle this problem head on through worldwide human rights initiatives such as The International Bill of Human Rights. The irony is that while the U.N. fights for women's rights, its globalist ideology is fueling the sex- trade, thus, actually causing more women to resort to prostitution. Women's rights groups, born out of the need to protest the grand right-wing conservative establishment, have over-compensated in some ways. This sort of "protestant" ideology has regretfully backfired on women, men, and mostly children due, in part, to the Far-Right's underlying philosophy: "if you can't beat 'em, join 'em in bringing ruin upon themselves."

Sadly, the biggest loss to society arising from the radical feminist movement may very well be a considerable segment of the upcoming generation. This could bring much more than we can handle, in that they, not being nurtured, cared for, and loved as in previous generations, would be most prone to dishing back that lack of love in many ways.

The fact that women have for so long been ostracized and segregated as second class beings by the rightist-Church gave birth to an extreme-leftist consciousness which ended up over-compensating. By turning to a matriarchal society in many ways, some gender inequalities which were existent prior to the 1960s in the U.S. are now severely over-compensated for. This explains why the witchcraft-centered "Mother nature" or "Mother earth" goddess has become such an extreme leftist-oriented political issue of our day. From the beginning of time, man has believed in the pagan gods and goddesses of the earth and these nature-based deities are among those condemned in the Bible. (Curiously, it has been the right-wing oil tycoons who have caused the bulk of the geological harm to the planet. The Far-Right is the primary offender of the earth, and is, therefore, provoking God Almighty. As Revelations 11:18 reveals, God will *"destroy those who destroy the earth."* It is very righteous indeed to protect the natural beauty of the world which the Far-Right is notoriously known for destroying, but again, to over-compensate in actually denouncing the creator – God – and adhering to the earth deities or goddess theology is to go overboard.)

While Mary, mother of Jesus, has been over-glorified, many women of the Bible have not received their much deserved credit (ie: Bathsheba, Hannah, Ruth). They have been ignored by the Far-Right for many centuries. Women should be respected, loved and cherished. They deserve to be heard, to have their say, to participate in decision making, to be appreciated for their unique God-given abilities, as man has his unique abilities. Man and woman were designed in a particular way, for a particular reason. For example, women were given nurturing qualities which are by and large absent in men, while men were given conquering qualities mostly lacking in women – those needed, say, to be on the front lines of a war, where a woman does not belong. Not that this supports a chauvinist mentality in the least, but there needs to be a limit as to what a man or woman should or should not do. These limits may be interpreted as "traditional" by radical feminists, but some traditions need to be preserved. Though outdated to many women, various conservative beliefs are in line with Biblical doctrine. Righteous conservatism has good points which deserve credit. The Apostle Paul writes a great deal on this issue in the New Testament from a rather conservative perspective.

Throughout time it has been the norm for the man to be the "head of household," and this has usually worked out quite well. However, if a man can allow the woman to "run the show" and this arrangement works for both of them, so be it. Many women, however, are losing their God-given role in promoting any sort of domestic "flip-flop."

The women's movement, then, has had some very negative repercussions for society at large. If a woman is single, the Biblical precepts may have some limits. Although I applaud the fact that women have made great strides against the Far-Right, when a woman is either married or a mother, the extreme leftist philosophy has proven to be much too overwhelming – thanks to the fact that it is ultimately Satan who exploits women through radical theories and movements.

Radical feminism has been as a demon to the fabric of society, especially since it is from here that the family unit began to crumble right out from under us. Though a "family" is differently interpreted by different people today, it has historically meant a man and his wife or wives and their offspring. In Biblical times, various concubines were also considered part of the family (Ecclesiastes 2:8). Very calculatingly, the globalists, who took advantage of this "woman of the future," knew quite well that by planting the seeds of change, we would change too much. In the name of equality, Satan has politicized this issue until practically making the girl or woman unequal in the opposite direction. One example of this over-compensation was illustrated by the conservative writer, Christina Hoff-Sommers in her book, *"The War Against Boys."* In it she attacked the extreme feminist myth that girls are still disadvantaged educationally and proved totally the opposite: it is now boys who are at a disadvantage. The scales have tilted in the opposite direction (partly due to the secular educational system). The extreme leftist end of the media, in particular the numerous talk shows which are being used more than ever before to promote male bashing, reveal that there are hidden agendas at this end of the spectrum too. It is only obvious to see that the reason why these shows use real losers and chauvinist pigs as a means to bash males in general is due to a massive objective to degrade the male while stirring up female hostility. This is just another extreme leftist tactic used by the globalists to "divide and conquer." How common it is these days to hear a woman say, "I don't need a man." To see our divorce rate rise to over fifty percent, is to see the byproduct of these changes. To see masses of children being raised by the local day care center is yet another by-product, with extremely disturbing repercussions for the future of society. When the woman has to attempt two full-time jobs (mothering and a career), neither will be done well, so society loses from both ends. Since the woman has to put her career before her children, she often feels as though she is not doing a good job at either. To take "Mommy" and turn her into full-time career woman, is to take her primary role and make it secondary. When this occurs, her children become secondary, which further erodes society in general. Thus, a domino effect toward a wicked society where everything is "upside down," a modern day rationale used by both extremes. There is nothing more important to man's adversary (Satan) than to destroy the divine family unit from within. While this happens the children are placed on the back burner – a win-win scenario for the evil empire. This echoes the method of operation used long ago in the garden of Eden when there too, Satan targeted the woman to entice, coerce, and control in order to ruin God's creations (Genesis 3; 1 Timothy 2:14). The present day feminine-oriented establishment is eerily similar to the goddess- oriented cultures of long ago. For a man to bow to a goddess is a delight for the evil empire, but an extreme abomination for God. What fitting parallel role does the Church play here? As a result of the highly revered Mary, this notion of the goddess-influenced society of the Babylonians falls in place as a hand in a glove (Babylonian Semiramis, Egyptian Isis). The Vatican honors these ancient goddesses immensely (an example of the Far-Left being under the influence of the Far-Right). A great painting of Isis on a throne, for example, is among the Vatican's prized possessions. The fact that Rome welcomes and promotes goddess-worship, as did the Cannanites, should make Catholic people wonder if the worship and apparitions of Mary are indeed "Godly."

In contrast to the scriptures, Mary has surpassed practically all other Biblical characters as the most universal figure. Throughout the globe, she has been glorified as no other woman, placed on the pedestal and throne equal to God. Is this Satan's crafty and deceptive work? 2 Thessalonians 2:9-10 clearly reflects this: *"The coming of the lawless one by the activity of Satan will be with all power and with (pretended) signs and wonders, and with all wicked deception for those who are to perish, because they refused to love the truth and so be saved."* Many "counterfeit appearances" of Mary are actually a world-wide effort by Satan to deceive the masses. As of the day of her death and in accordance with Biblical doctrine, Mary is as dead as every other person who has ever passed away. She is asleep and awaiting her "day in court" – that great and final judgement day – like everyone else. She has a larger following in some countries than even Christ, which sounds like a maneuver of anti-Christ. By the deification of Mary, the masses relegate attention and authority away from he who should be getting it: God. It is interesting to note the depths to which modern culture has inculcated the honor of Mary into our psyche as is the case in American football: "Hail Mary touchdown pass." Yet another example was seen in the famous Beatles song *"Let it be"*- lyrics which glorify the worship of this mothergoddess. This should not come as much of a surprise, since often music is another medium Satan specializes in to infiltrate the minds of the masses. Music can be a sort of hypnotizing tool which numbs the mind through repetitive lyrics. This, in turn, subjects the mind to evil. Incidentally, I do not see how repeating "Hail Mary's" over and over and over again, as is taught by the Church (ie: the rosary), helps to redeem us of our sins – the use of "prayer beads" was actually incorporated into Catholicism via the Hindu religion. Was that not the reason Christ shed his blood – as predicted in the Old Testament, especially in Isaiah 53? See also Matthew 6:7. [Note: "Lady Justice" also gives homage to Egyptian, Greek, and Roman goddesses.]

THE HOMOSEXUAL MOVEMENT AND THE SEXUAL REVOLUTION
Another of these very powerful political groups now influencing the entire world as a formidable cult is the homosexual powerhouse which is such a lobbying force that politicians, including of course, the Catholic Church itself and staunch right-wingers, have been courting these groups. Hence, a 180 degree turnaround in what is now acceptable as the norm. A man or woman who engages in homosexual acts with another consenting adult in the confines of his or her home should be free to do so – thus, one should mind one's own business. This is a two-way street though. This libertarian view of "live and let live" is very much in line with Biblical teachings, though it is good to show our fellow man what the Bible says in a gentle manner. The gay community should indeed be protected by the enactment of hate-crime laws, as no one has a right to assault another because of his or her sexual preference. The exceptions would be: the rapist, the child molester, and those who have anything to do with the production, promotion, or distribution of child pornography. The latter two should commit suicide – see Matthew 18:5-6. Our justice system has oftentimes been much too lenient with those

convicted of molesting children, including many "priests."
The judgmental Far-Right should heed the warning that they
will be judged by their own harsh standards one day, for God will not
judge all by the same means, and to throw stones now is to be stoned
later. It is generally not good to judge another, unless you are per-
forming your worldly duties as a judge or juror, but it is Christ-like
to defend the faith without forcing it on others or "throwing stones"
at sinners. When either the extreme right attempts to legislate its
morality and force their views on everyone else or the extreme left
legislates for its "rights" and forces its agenda as politically correct,
the end result will be a twisted society where either the "Hitler-izing"
of society ensues or the feminizing of men (and vice-versa) become
commonplace, as in the extreme left. This extreme is just part of the
larger diabolical goal: to alter and destroy God's creations by taking
the exclusively male characteristics out of the male and the unique
female characteristics out of the female – an abomination of the highest order. According to the Bible, it is not for men to wear women's
clothing or women to wear men's, either. Deuteronomy 22:5: *"A
woman shall not wear anything that pertains to a man, nor shall a
man put on a woman's garment, for whoever does these things is an
abomination to the Lord your God."* The two angels who destroyed
the sleazy-Sodom and grotesque- Gomorrah would certainly concur
with this logic (Genesis chapter 19). Both Old and New Testaments
are in accordance on this really basic issue of homosexuality: Leviticus 20:13 and Roman 1:26-29.

Some homosexuals, however, are victims of incest. Then there
are those who were in heterosexual relationships or marriages that
failed, so they "went the other way." Still others are partly victims of
societal changes which have been accepting, condoning, and in many
cases promoting homosexuality. Will God allow some homosexuals
into his kingdom? What about bi-sexuals, hermaphrodites, prostitutes, or criminals? Who can truly judge another as not being worthy? The Judges of mankind may allow numerous people which man
deems "undesirable" to enter the kingdom. As to homosexuals, maybe
biological issues such as an excess of either testosterone or estrogen
will be considered. Perhaps The Judges will judge them and find that

among many, there have been circumstantial issues which inclined a person toward a particular lifestyle or even toward crime. We know, however, that according to the scriptures, homosexuality is an abomination. If God never changes and is the same yesterday, today, and tomorrow, unlike the Church which supposedly represents him, it is fair to conclude that the next garden of Eden, paradise, or heaven will be reminiscent of the first – one made up of heterosexual "Adams" and "Eves." From the very beginning, in Genesis 2:18, when God saw that the recently created man was "lonely," he made him a beautiful female to be his mate and lover. To mix this sexual issue around in any way is to diametrically oppose the very basics of human physiology which God created to be used in a specific manner. For many, the notion of two women engaging in some sort of intimate display of affection (as obviously they cannot have penetrating sex) is more tolerable than two men who engage in any form of homosexual activity.

While the Boy Scouts of America defend their faith, policy, and right to place only heterosexuals in their club, the extreme left has argued that this American institution is discriminating against them (as was in a high-profile case arising out of Oak Park, Illinois). The homosexuals were plain wrong. If they were not accepted in this institution, why should their agenda be forced upon everyone else through the mandates of a court? Is that not also legislating for another brand of morality? The homosexuals should mind their own business and not trample on the beliefs of others, either. They have often crossed that fine line and become much too brazen in their demands to be included where they are excluded or to be legally declared a "married couple" with all the benefits afforded heterosexuals.

No one but God has a right to condemn, but we who are not led astray by extremist philosophies (in not giving in to "upside down" reasoning) do not have to condone legislative motions which would completely alter today's family unit even more than what radical feminism has done. The National Association of Catholic Diocesan Lesbian and Gay Ministries is a prime example of the leftist radicals within, yet in conflict with the Church, who would surely disagree.

While priests and nuns have been forced to follow the celibate orders of the Church, many have, not surprisingly, turned to the same sex. Ironically, various states have laws which make "sodomy" illegal. The Apostle Paul said *"deacons and bishops"* are to have *"one wife"* -see 1 Timothy 3.

PROMISCUITY:
THE OTHER BYPRODUCT OF THE SEXUAL REVOLUTION
Promiscuity, which multiplied after the 1960's, has brought too much freedom for some, as it is no longer a shame, for women in particular, to have various sexual mates. Not that it is right for a man to be a "whore," but there was never much of a negative stigma attached to a man who slept with various women. Men, however, who make a hobby out of impregnating women and abandoning them need to seriously look at how wrong that is. For anyone, male or female, to sleep around with all sorts of people is to give in to the flesh without discerning the spirit, a strong point of the Apostle Paul throughout his New Testament writings.

PORNOGRAPHY
Pornography, which is now a multi-billion dollar a year industry, has been primarily a product of the extreme left, but as is the case with other big-money industries, the right puts aside its conservatism when it comes to profit. We may be "slouching toward Gomorrah," but clearly the right is collaborating in our demise. Fact is, some conservative corporations have reaped large sums of money from pornography. Satan has again done the "flip-flop"- he has cheapened, degraded, and trashed the God-given beauty of human sexuality. Pornography is primarily an attack on women, reducing them to a piece of meat. If some adults want to watch smut, however, they should be free to do so.

THE EXTREME SECULAR ESTABLISHMENT
This leftist entity is also very much infiltrated by rightist dogma, as in the "discovery" of America by Christopher Columbus which is commonly taught throughout the world. The sole reason why this is

deemed factual is due to the underlying racism which is meshed into the most basic lessons which are taught to the young. Is it a wonder that throughout the last century one has been deemed "smart" or "educated" depending on the knowledge and memory one retains of Western European people, history, the arts, etc.? This establishment, ultimately governed by the U.N. World Core Curriculum (Kah, Ch.7), is another evil which has been "Darwin-izing" and derailing many for decades. The masses have been taught the far-fetched notion that mankind evolved from some sort of monkey millions and millions of years ago. This diabolic explanation is simply another medium taken by the evil empire to cause as many educated folk to conclude that that which is actually demonic in origin is good and feasible and what is good and feasible (ie: creationism) is not feasible, thus, erroneous. This will inadvertently serve the Far-Right in justifying that their "Christianity" be taught in today's schools. Public school prayer is discussed later.

This establishment has been endangering the world's youth through its radical new- age philosophies as the globalists focus on the "dumbing down" of the upcoming lower and middle classes, partly via a barrage of new testing standards. There is no doubt that the poor and minorities are the initial 'fall guys' as various recent studies have shown. One can easily see the objective to teach the young all sorts of evil as is clear by what the material used today entails: horror and violence related books and movies – as are those very popular ones which promote sorcery and witchcraft. Though I am not advocating banning these books or movies, their wicked nature should not be part of the curriculum in the public schools. America has basically integrated Halloween, a festival which honors wickedness at its core, into its everyday teachings. Then we wonder when a child, usually a male, reacts violently to the garbage his mind is subjected to. Since males are more prone to violence, these books are of considerable influence particularly to boys. To some, the content of these books may seem trivial, but then that is just the way man's adversary (Satan) wants man to think; by erasing the fine line which separates good from bad, the bad becomes unidentifiable, which leads to severe spiritual drought and decay. The secular establishment is no doubt under the control of the globalist clan who is using any and every manner to further destabilize the whole of American culture. Very clearly, these books are more popular to kids than reading books of substance, valor, and righteousness – books which do not veer too far to the right or to the left. America is basically being set up to eventually fail, and this is merely one example. Regretfully, the dedication of thousands of under-paid teachers, particularly in the inner-cities, is to some extent, in vain.

HOLLYWOOD
We should be very wary of the rising Religious Right with its big money, political influence, and potentially dangerous brainwashing of the masses via a wave of "Christian" films and headline theology which are likely to continue being produced in the near future. The close ties between the Democratic Party and the not-always-leftist entertainment industry reduces the integrity of that party since it is Hollywood which is often a haven for extremist ideology. But in light of the massive money machine which has empowered the Republican Party, the democrats have been put in a predicament where they too, must seek out funding from a variety of entities to cover their overhead.

Though there is great entertainment which comes from Hollywood, there is also plenty which demoralizes and destroys the spirit and the mind, particularly of the younger generations. From the movie industry to some of the hard rap and metal / hard rock, Satan, being the prince of visual and audible enticements, does indeed use entertainment as a seductive tool to manipulate the young and the masses who are vulnerable to his ploys. Part of the New York and Hollywood music industry which is promoting music, if it deserves to be called such, that actually hypnotizes the mind and subjects it to the demonic realm is a major influence which pollutes to the core. For decades even some of the most famous artists have also glorified the use, and even worse, the abuse of drugs. In more recent times some have pushed their limits in promoting hatred and even violence toward women.

The conservatives have a strong selling point when it comes to the delicate issue of censorship. The escalation of trash instilled in a our mind and soul would cause any "moral" person to contemplate the need for some sort of censorship (though I am not suggesting this is necessarily the answer). This is a prime example of how Satan unleashes his extreme leftist perversions to warrant the extreme rightist reactions on the part of the masses which in turn give way to the intrusion of "new age" policies.

A variety of high quality films have come from the movie industry in the past which deserve praise (ie:"*The Mission*" with Robert De'niro) in that they have a worthwhile message, not necessarily liberal or conservative, either. This has been declining, however, as the demand for not-so-wholesome movies has risen, thus, cheapening America's standards and eroding decency – just another "supply and demand" issue. Generating this sort of demand was a top priority for those who gain from the overall social decline of America. Once the ball is rolling downhill, it will roll by itself until hitting rock bottom.

Curiously enough, by Hollywood and Disney promoting homosexuality as being good and generating wider acceptance, they have inadvertently fueled the fire of AIDS here and in many countries, since so much of the world is caught up in the American music and movie industry. And then it is the humanitarian end of Hollywood who in turn aids those afflicted through many a fundraiser – an endless cycle seems to be the case here. Some have alleged that AIDS and Ebola are God's punishment for the immorality of homosexuals. Others assert that they are man-made diseases which were created to rid the earth of homosexuals. While others claim that it is a racist conspiracy targeting those of African origin and other minorities. The masses may never know until God himself reveals the truth, but if either of the latter two are true, it is not too difficult to conclude that the Far-Right is responsible.

Though it is fabulous to see white British rock musicians joining black American Rap stars, there remains a great deal of racism within the entire entertainment business, in particular the movie industry. Hollywood has done little to promote the cause of minorities. There are still relatively few "super-heroes" of Hispanic, African, Indian,

Oriental, or Arabic descent which children of these groups can look up to. Ultimately, many of these kids emulate only white super-stars – just the way the Far-Right wants. I have nothing at all against whites being super-stars. I am merely expressing the fact that the above stated is not coincidence. It is a deliberate attempt to lessen those who are not white. It is interesting how the vast majority of "good guys" in the movie industry are not surprisingly non-Hispanic whites. Peculiarly so, minorities often get the "bad guy" roles which only serve to stereotype and fuel what the Far-Right is longing for: to have the white race portrayed as being superior to all others. The effects are so mind-boggling that the vulnerable among minorities will go to great lengths to "whiten" themselves, denying their origins by aiding in down-grading, criticizing, condemning, and castigating their own people, culture, and genealogy. Some of these victims actually serve the interests of the racist extreme right in furthering the subjugation of all minorities by serving as a pawn or puppet. It is these who feel that to go along with the program, even if that very program is se-verely suppressing their own, is to do right, maybe "extreme right." Well, it is more than just wrong, it is fundamentally contrary to the progress of one's own people. While there is nothing wrong with assimilation in the name of progress, to progress to the point of di-vorcing one's roots and serving in a war against your own is to take two steps forward and three backward. To disgrace one's origins is to disgrace one's self – exactly how the Far-Right makes "wolves in sheep's clothing" out of some minorities. The racist right is even present within some of the Hispanic media. This trend surely has been influenced by numerous Latin American mergers and acquisi-tions with Spain and other European countries in the last few years.

HOLLYWOOD AND THE YOUNG
The lack of discretion toward the young in the movie industry cou-pled with the obsession for big profit makes the cultural impact, a severe desensitizing of the young, an extremely negative one which deserves a great deal of attention. Hollywood does have its take in the fact that the globalists are using it to gain more ground over America by creating all sorts of dysfunction and division from within.

The overall lack of respect toward adults by children and teens who are subliminally affected by the severely lowered standards which are now the norm is quite prevalent. Many parents, with good reason, feel a sense of losing their children to this modern-day vile culture which fuels the degradation of the young, thus, paving the way for a weaker and susceptible future generation. It is so common to see the disgusting manner in which too many youngsters speak to their parents these days, in part, a result of the lack of respect toward parents which today's culture instills in children from a very young age (see Ephesians 6:1-3). In doing this severe psychological harm to children, conflicts arise as a result of the child reacting as an equal to his or her parents. It is my contention that a spanking is not only warranted and good, but to fail to reprimand them, which sometimes requires reasonable corporeal punishment, is wicked and evil – see in Proverbs 23:13-14. Sometimes a good spanking is "in the best interests of the child."

DEBT AND THE "MILKING OF AMERICA"

Debt, which often comes from one tilting too far to the left (as in "overspending"), is a wicked and evil curse which is exactly what is happening to America and much of the world. This hemisphere, which is undergoing a new "inquisition," is being subdued by the debt which the globalists have used as a weapon on a grand scale. More than ever before, we live in a credit oriented society which wants everything now. The fast pace to "keep up with the Jones's" is not only making the globalist clans much richer through their severe usury of the masses, but it is making the average American who gets in debt, poorer. Fact is, America is getting "milked" by the overpowering globalists in numerous ways (ie: excessive interest), as it is first through the economy that they over-run a country and second through its legal system. As of the 1980's they have "turned up the heat" and we have entered phase two. The average American small business has often been "taken to the cleaners" by those who have one objective: to take out and take over. Bankruptcies are likely to continue rising for not only middle America, but even giants like K-Mart. The term monopoly is most appropriate in this day and new age.

Slowly but surely, we are being chewed up by this material world and the rampant covetousness which the globalists profit handsomely from. By Satan keeping us in the bondage of debt, his disciples gain more ground – while the poor, working class, and middle America pay the price.

SELECTED CREDITS

El Tiempo, Olga Lucia Lozano y Juanita Leon, *"Los 7 pecados capitales de la Iglesia" – "The 7 capital sins of the Church,"* Bogota, Colombia – Domingo 28 de Febrero / Sunday 28th of February, 1999. {Abuso de Mujeres en el Pasado / Abuse of Women in the Past}

The Tampa Tribune, Raf Casert and Paul Shepard of The Associated Press, *"Sex Trafficking Is A Multibillion-Dollar Industry,"* Sunday, November 25, 2001.

Time Magazine, Jeffrey Kluger, *"Special Report, Global Warming: A Climate of Despair,"* April 9, 2001.

U.S. News & World Report, *"The Pope's Cardinal – Roger Mahony Mixes Politics and Piety,"* January 25, 1999. {Gay and Lesbian Diocese}

International Herald Tribune / The Associated Press, *"Quietly Aids Kills Priests – Hundreds Die in Solitude,"* Paris, France, January 31, 2000.

Leonard G. Horowitz, DMD., *"Emerging Viruses: Aids and Ebola, Nature, Accident, or Intentional?"* Rockport, MA: Tetrahedron, Inc., 1997.

The Associated Press, George Mwangi, *"AIDS Overtakes War as African Killer,"* Kenya, Nairobi, July 22, 1999

St. Petersburg Times / Atlanta, *"Minorities Have Most New HIV Infections,"* Wednesday, October, 2000.

The Nation, Salih Booker and William Minter, *"Aids and The New World Order, Global Apartheid,"* July 9, 2001.

New York Times / The Tampa Tribune, Money & Business Section H , *"Corporate Mainstays Profiting from Porn,"* Sunday October 29, 2000.

Gary H. Kah, *"The New World Religion."* Noblesville, Indiana: Hope International Publishing, Inc., 1998. {U.N. World Core Curriculum}

The Tampa Tribune, Parade, *"Is Illiteracy Dooming the Next Generation as Well?"* Sunday, November 25, 2001.

Hispanic Magazine, Raul Yzaguirre, *"Census Shows Disparity in Education of Latino Children,"* April 2001.

The Tampa Tribune, Metro, *"West Palm Beach – Wealthy Students Do Best on FCAT, Analysis Shows,"* December 23, 2001.

Robert H. Bork, *"Slouching toward Gomorrah."* New York: Regan Books, 1996.

Scripps Howard News Service, *"Hispanics Press Networks For More Time,"* 2000.

Latin Trade Magazine, Mike Zellner, Miami; Raymond Colit, Sao Paulo, *"The Spanish Acquisition: The Final Adventure,"* April 2001. {The Last Inquisition}

Time Magazine, Nancy Gibbs, *"Do Kids Have Too Much Power?"* August 6, 2001.

CHAPTER THREE

PART 1

FAR-RIGHT POLITICS IN AMERICA
AND WELFARE REFORM

The inevitable "separation" between Church and State has allowed for those of other faiths to have the basic right to equal protection under the law – a truly great idea. The law itself, however, when it is fundamentally rooted in a "Christian" order (as is the United States), can never truly and completely separate itself from the state. In retrospect, one can ask, "how can the state, founded on strictly conservative values, dismiss the Church who brought the values and yet remain a state distinct from religious influence?" It cannot. This separation, then, was just that – a separation, not a "divorce," as many would assume. Our legal system, rooted in Latin or in other words of the right, will continue to be ruled by the same regardless of the influx of even radical religious diversity and tolerance for the beliefs of others. It is worth noting, for example, that our legal system still carries on the traditional Red Mass – an annual convention of lawyers and judges to seek out God's blessings and reaffirm their oaths in, not surprisingly, a Catholic Church. The Roman empire's political framework was and remains inherently the origin of our legal system and social order no matter how far some think or claim we have become independent of the Church.

As is commonly known, many of the empire's beliefs have historically upheld racist propaganda which is still very much a part of the political infra-structure despite the efforts of many good liberal (and some conservative) people to integrate people of all races into higher government. The fact that the vast majority of lawyers, judges, and politicians are still non-Hispanic white males is clear and convincing evidence that the "sidelining" of minorities – and women in the past, by the Far-Right, will continue to be with us. Why? Because the right-wing will not accept too many minorities in roles where they are in any considerable position of authority. In subjugating minorities to a great extent, the laws of the land remain more inclined to the opinions and beliefs of non- Hispanic whites since they continue to be the most influential segment of the white race with legislative power (not to mention judicial and executive). The fact that our criminal justice system incarcerates blacks and Hispanics at an alarming rate in comparison to non- Hispanic whites is not merely coincidental. It is a repercussion of the laws which are passed by the non-Hispanic white majority. According to The Associated Press, 1 in 32 adults is now in the corrections system. Due process is affected by these complex issues, as there remains a large shadow of the racist ways of yesterday inherent in the whole of man's brand of justice.

Though the great U.S. Constitution provides that we are all equal under the law, we need to keep in mind what law, man's Roman-derived law. It has been, is, and will continue to be a "Latin system of law" which in conjunction with economic factors that also lean toward the white privileged non-Hispanic male overall, the reality is that not much has really changed since the Roman Empire of Christ's day. 1 Corinthians 6:1 clearly declares the Roman legal system as "unrighteous."

The very righteous efforts of numerous liberal politicians have been instrumental in bringing some equality as to these and other complex issues. Since we are a "Republi-crat" state (this term itself is dominated by the right), the Far-Right will dominate the state. The rotten Far-Right always seeks to rot a substantial part of the left, making some of the left puppets of rightist dogma. Our system of government, being under the influence of the Globalist New World Order ultra-elitists, has been gradually reshaping the political infra-structure of this country toward a Far-Right dominated establishment. Although "politically correct" on the surface, it is extremely anti-Biblical at heart. The Far-Right, where the bulk of big-money is, is becoming exceedingly over-bearing on a global level. Since power is money and vice-versa, then those who have it abundantly will not only make sure they keep it, but they will make sure that those who have less will have even less – typical ultra-rightist avaricious philosophy. It is by going down a similar road that entire countries which have experienced the hardened right hand of Rome in the past have reached a point where the tyrannical state leaves only revolution as the recourse available to the masses. This is what the globalists are awaiting in order to usher in their "New World Order." I am certainly not advocating for revolutionary measures to be taken by anyone, as what is prophesied to occur no one can stop from unraveling at its due time even for one second; and it is apparent that the Biblical "revelations" and "messages" reserved for the end times are being revealed these days as foretold in Daniel 12:4. On this note, it is fitting to point out Romans 13 which in essence explains that it is ultimately God who has a grip on this world's governing authorities, as it is he who allows even evil to temporarily prevail. We must remember that until Christ is sent back here by his Father, all governing authorities fall short of being truly "righteous." We should humble ourselves and pray for those who govern over us as the Bible instructs us to do – may God be with them. Christ, upon receiving the death penalty, did not lead others to revolt, but went to be slaughtered as was his destiny. This, however, should not be misconstrued, for there is a time and place to defend one's self.

WELFARE REFORM

Note: In the upcoming section, I am not launching an offensive against the rich. I am defending thousands against the attacks of those who are rich in evil – as in those who are on the offensive against the poor and middle class at large. It is highly likely that some of the rich in this world will indeed enter the kingdom as they are deemed worthy. Christ never said that all rich men would be doomed to hell – nor did he assure a poor man a green light, either. His messages though, were by and large for the "underdog," the meek, and the humble – not attributes which one finds among many of the ultra-wealthy or those who rob the average American (ie: the Enron crooks).

Though the response to the victims of the September 11, 2001 tragedy was truly Christ-like as America reacted with great generosity and a genuinely humane spirit, a hardening of the heart toward the needy has been taking place for some time now. We should not forget the impoverished people of Afghanistan, and throughout the world, as their plight is surely beyond our imagination. America's interest in the poor and general social assistance / social security to those in need over the past fifteen years or so, has been severely declining for a variety of reasons. Since charitable donations fluctuate in the U.S., many feel that charity can effectively replace the gaps left by welfare reform. This could not be further from the truth. It is imperative to note that the ultimate goal of the Far-Right has not been to reform but to abolish the "welfare state." Among today's complex political issues, assistance to the poor crosses over heavily into Biblical doctrine. Fact is, in the wealthiest country of the world, the U.S., there is a growing number of poor literally ending up on the streets. In the long run, there is a very clear threat of leaving many more thousands of Americans homeless and hopeless despite recent trends of unity in America.

I wholeheartedly applaud the British musician, Phil Collins, who brought to the forefront the plight of the ultra-poor in his famous song, *"Just another day in paradise"* some years ago. Another "Brit" I applaud for having a great and warm heart was Princess Diana. Ralph Nader, who has been quite outspoken about corporate welfare, deserves much credit too, as this helps educate the tax-payer who is being fleeced by big government and big business, not by the poor. As usual, the Far-Right does not want too much of the truth to come out, so it is good politics to keep the focus elsewhere: on those who are vulnerable, weak, and powerless. It should come as no surprise to the reader by now that it is my intention to also correlate the injustice and merciless heart of the Far- Right with the multiplication of poverty and hunger in the United States and throughout the world. To them, I would strongly urge to remember that Christ, being symbolized as a lowly lamb, born amongst typical working class poor, will come back to dish out his superior brand of final justice. Then he will not be of the lowly or humble poor, for he will return as a fierce and very powerful lion.

The following is partly in honor of Franklin D. Roosevelt who was a true humanitarian with a heart of gold:

As has been the case for over a decade, the negative sentiments toward the poor and lower classes by the middle and upper classes produced not a "kinder and gentler nation" but a "harsh, bitter and divided" nation in this respect. This division is another part of an integral plan to change the face of America by way of the globalist hierarchies. By selling the mid-upper classes on the notion that the poor are costing them too much, a further erosion of justice, mercy, and decency has certainly been multiplying since the early eighties when the right turned the spotlight on the poor. The mid-upper classes have been impregnated by a seed which is the product of massive propaganda that has projected everyone receiving financial assistance as being no-good-bums who just want to prey on the public and "take the system for a ride." Though there are those who fall into this category, the fact is, America has been sold on anti-Biblical, anti-liberal, extreme rightist dogma which could have very negative (karmic-like) consequences in the not-too-distant future. It is in essence a divisive seed which when cultivated is meant to cause great inner turmoil within all economic classes, particularly between the lower and middle echelons – pitting one against the other as seen in Galatians 5:15. It is no surprise that a large percent of the "welfare recipients" who prey on the taxpayer are oftentimes mega-wealthy right-wing corporations, who through their lobbying power, finance and enhance extreme conservative views. For these, being wealthy and powerful is not enough, they must profit from the poor and lower classes while "throwing stones" and subjecting the most vulnerable (the elderly, orphans, single parents, and the disabled) to attacks by even Christians, liberals, and democrats – again, the epitomy of right-wing greed and hypocrisy. Their underlying motto is basically "steal from the poor to give to the rich." But to look closer at the severity of this wicked machine, one may add, "and then kick 'em while they're down." This is what they mean by "have your cake and eat it too." One can therefore conclude, "and leave the crumbs on the floor for the poor, in the name of generosity." To pervert the many excerpts in the Bible which clearly call for justice, kindness, generosity, and mercy toward the poor is enough to make a truly good-spirited person realize that Satan is hard at work in bringing about a hardened heart toward the needy at large and regretfully the deserving poor. Conservative politicians would do well in following the example of Jim Jeffords who had the integrity to go against the flow of the hardened Far-Right.

Today's common term "bleeding heart liberal" used by many conservatives to mock the left, as though it were indecent to have a good heart, has been projected as a weakness, when it oftentimes shows totally the opposite: sheer inner strength. Ezekiel 36:26- *"A new heart I will give you, and a new spirit I will put within you; and I will take out of your flesh the heart of stone and give you one of flesh."* Luke 6:45 – *"The good man out of the treasure of his heart produces good, and the evil man out of his evil treasure produces evil; for out of the abundance of the heart his mouth speaks."* Those who have no heart for others who are worthy of receiving assistance will be judged in like manner by God and his Judges who will not judge everyone with equal compassion. Matthew 7:1-2- *"Judge not that you be not judged, for with the judgement you pronounce you will be judged, and the measure you give will be the measure you get."* Malachi 3:5 – *"Then I will draw near to you for judgement; I will be a swift witness against the sorcerers, against the adulterers, against those who swear falsely, against those who oppress the hireling in his wages, the widow and the orphan, against those who thrust aside the sojourner, and do not fear me."* It is God Almighty and Jesus Christ who are masters of "what comes around, goes around."

The following are more powerful (paraphrased) Biblical references which give substantial backing as to why it is an immense mistake to allow extreme right ideology to blossom and permeate one's heart, making it one of stone:

Leviticus 25:35-36 – If one's brother cannot support himself, we are to bring him "under our wing."

Deuteronomy 15:11- Since the poor will always exist, we are to generously give them a hand.

Deuteronomy 15:18 – We are to be kind to those who are indebted to us.

Deuteronomy 24:17 – We should not pervert the justice due the alien or the fatherless, but remember God redeemed the Israelites from the hard hearted Egypt.

Psalms 9:18 – The poor will not always be "put on the back burner."

Psalms 41:1 – He who brings aid to those in need will be blessed.

Proverbs 14:21 – He who hates is a sinner; he who gives to the poor will be content.

Proverbs 15:16 – It is better to live modestly with fear of the Lord than to have abundance with great troubles.

Proverbs 19:17 – Those who give to the poor are not forgotten by God's laws of retribution.

Proverbs 22:16 – Those who abuse the poor and profit by it or give to corporate welfare / tax breaks for the rich better watch out.

Proverbs 22:22-23 – To rob the poor or deny the alien is "bad karma."

Proverbs 29:7 – The righteous knows his moral duty to the poor, the wicked overlooks the needs of the less fortunate.

Ecclesiastes 5:8 – Do not be shocked to see the hierarchies suppressing the poor.

Ecclesiastes 5:10 – The love of money does not bring satisfaction.

Isaiah 10:1-2 – Woe to those who deny the widow and the fatherless their justice.

Isaiah 58:7-9 – Isn't it Christ-like to help the hungry, the homeless, the naked? If one does, God will hear his call.

Zechariah 7:9-14 – Render true judgments of mercy and kindness to the poor, or else!

Matthew10:42 – He who gives even a cup of cold water to a child will not be forgotten.

Matthew 18:5 – He who receives a poor child in Christ's name receives Christ himself.
*Matthew 25:35-36 – Christ himself was hungry, thirsty, a stranger, naked , sick and a prison inmate.
Mark 10:21- Christ tells a man who wants to "make it to heaven" to sell his belongings and give them to the poor.
John 13:34 – Love one another – the 11th commandment.
Philippians 2:4 – Paul tells those at Philippi to look after each others interests.
1 Timothy 5:8 – He who does not look after his own family is a scoundrel.
1 Timothy 6:17-19 – Those who are wealthy should not be conceited and arrogant or see money as the answer – they are to be "liberal and generous."
James 1:27 – Pure religion rests on having a heart toward the poor and keeping this world and its enticements at bay.

Throughout time there have been poor people, and it has always been wrong to give heed to doctrines of devils who sell their ideas on "positive pretexts" with severely negative hidden agendas which are derived from very "negative pretexts." The deserving poor need a hand, and to negate them this Biblically-based mandate is to go against Christ or in other words to become more like the "Anti-Christ." Anything which is contrary to Christ is obviously anti-Christ, as is the hardened right.

The Far-Right has grossly over-exemplified the following to their benefit in their massive propaganda against the poor at large: *"For even when we were with you, this we command you, that if any would not work, neither should they eat"* (2 Thessalonians 3:10). No doubt that those who can work, but want to abuse the generosity of the government, which has greatly decreased in recent years, need to "render to Caesar" and contribute to society. Although they are a minority among the poor, it is these who when offered a hand want to take an arm. Though sometimes they have been the product of generations on welfare and thus know of no other means of surviving, they who fall into this category of "plain lazy" do indeed need a change of attitude. Fact is, however, many "welfare recipients" want to work for their daily bread and not feel as beggars, bums, and outcasts. It should be noted that from the beginning of time, even those who do put in a full day's work need a hand from time to time. From the Appalachian poor to the ghettos of Los Angeles, there are folks of all races who should not be forgotten. Additionally, even the foreigner was never excluded from receiving aid in the scriptures.

Despite the fact that I agree it is time to be mildly conservative, again, we should be very cautious not to over-compensate. Those who claim to be righteous in passing laws which affect the sustenance of the powerless should be careful and mindful not to go overboard, for the repercussions will be dreadful. It is prudent to be fiscally conservative and not waste tax-payer funds; it is wrong, very wrong though, to turn our back when we are called upon to be kind, humane, and hospitable, for it may be that we are "entertaining angels unaware" (Hebrews 13:1-2). Many of the "weakest links" in society may very well be among these angels. Conversely, many of the "strongest links" may very well be demons.

We all need to come "back to our senses"- to condone idleness is wicked. For the Far-Right to apply this premise and sever the goodness of being humane and of social assistance toward those who cannot work, the truly needy, is much more than wicked. While many large cities liberally spend tax-payer funds to replace multi-million dollar, state of the art sports stadiums, low-middle income neighborhoods are brushed aside and left in shambles. The fine work of many democrats in the past regarding the truly needy is being ignored even by other democrats, creating a clear and present inclination toward abolishing the welfare state. Again, this is the ultimate goal of the globalists and their ultra-conservative partners in crime. This may be a popular idea, but that does not always translate to righteousness. "Social Darwinism" is absolutely anti-Christ.

To make the poor among the first targets of fiscal reforms is disgraceful in that there is massive waste throughout big government which is screaming for reform. Additionally, it is beyond hypocritical that while many politicians, some democrats included, live as kings on public funding, they have the nerve to attack the deserving poor for collecting their rather insignificant portion. The audacity of some politicians to use public tax dollars to feather their own nests in many different ways is the epitome of hypocrisy (ie: public service announcements which again, are to explain to the masses what is "in their best interests"). Many of these politicians are compassionate – toward the rich. Americans should never forget that these social assistance programs were created and preserved by some fine democrats of outstanding moral character to keep widows and children, among others, from virtually being homeless and destitute, irrelevant of religion. In the coming years, should the economy not rebound, and it may not, there will be a growing number of people who will need government unemployment benefits, welfare, handouts, and charity. Will they be stigmatized as leeches too?

Unlike God, man looks on the outward appearances, reducing those who are not "cosmopolitan" while elevating those who are chic, hip, and attractive (1 Samuel 16:7). Since the poor are often judged by their appearances, as they lack funds for beautiful homes, fine clothes, and nice cars, society would do well to absorb John 7:24, *"Do not judge by appearances..."*

A brief note on the Church and the poor: Though the humanitarian missions of great people like Mother Teresa are certainly praiseworthy, it is little consolation when Catholic Charities attempt to fill gaps with respect to the plight of the poor when to a great extent it is the hierarchies within the Vatican and their globalist colleagues who are responsible for much of the depravity. It is preposterous to see how many good Catholics are being made a mockery of by their own Church in trying to mend the wrongs created by their superiors and associates throughout the world.

PART 2

THE RIGHT-WING'S REVIVAL AND THE "WAR ON DRUGS"

Certainly, Ronald Reagan will go down in history as a great actor and President, as there were some good things which he did for this nation. The right, though, has also had its share of controversy. The fact that it has been known to ignore human rights abuses throughout the globe in pursuit of its agendas, as was done in Central America during the 1980's, is but one example. Some have expressed great concerns that "the war on terrorism" will be used as a selling point to further human rights violations in the future – this is highly likely.

Many feel that with the controversial 2000 win of George W. Bush as the President of the United States, it is clear that "big-money" has made its largest leap. The revival of what Ronald Reagan began, is back on track (ie: welfare for their corporate pals and big tax breaks for their big-time buddies which was sold to the people under the "upside down" method). Other areas of interest to many liberals and some conservatives include excessive Nasa and defense spending. For this, the staunch conservatives are quite the "liberal spendthrifts." I am not suggesting layoffs per se, but really, does knowing the atmospheric conditions of Pluto warrant the massive amounts spent when we have public schools in this country that are falling apart? Since the aeronautic corporations charge the Pentagon such exorbitant fees, perhaps a little "reform" would do the tax-payer some justice. As to our military, few would argue that it is prudent to have a strong defense. However, it is a fact that this country has at times "over-compensated" for any lack of preparedness or high-tech weaponry which is why the tax-payer is now expected to foot the bill to dispose of stockpiles of weapons of mass destruction.

Many assert that the G.O.P. is comprised of racists who are indifferent, at best, toward minorities. This may not be just rhetoric from the left, as there is a series of issues which give some credibility to this position. Through the massive appointing of primarily conservative, non-Hispanic white Catholic judges by the Reagan and Bush administrations, this nation was shoved into "legal conservatism" which brought with it a great deal of repressive legislation. This, by the way, was a primary reason for Bill Clinton's more centrist position during his two terms. Did the 2000 election serve to suppress liberals and minorities even more? The thousands of Floridians whose votes were not counted, for the plethora of reasons which eventually swayed the courts, certainly had a valid complaint. As it stands, many have analyzed and studied in depth the overall process of voting and concluded the process is inclined toward favoring the inclusion of higher echelons over lower echelons, white-collar over blue-collar, and whites over minorities – all factors which only the Far-Right with all their political might would find beneficial to their objectives. The debacle which the Democratic Party suffered is one of considerable proportions, as it is democracy itself which is threatened- a democracy which is being altered by the globalists on both extremities. The "upside down 'legalistic' logic" (arguments formulated to resonate as making perfect sense, yet are highly unjust and unfair) and typical ultra-rightist impatience used by Bush's legal dream team were nothing more than another show of when that which is flat out wrong is manifested, perceived, pushed, and concluded as right. It was clear that to allow democracy to prevail, a complete recount would have been the only real way to accomplish this goal. From a simply democratic perspective, when the last vote is tallied, he who has the most votes wins. Seeing an opportunity to manipulate the democratic process, the right "turned up the heat" and via the media, sold their dispute to the U.S. Supreme Court and much of the nation. This twisted, upside down manner of selling a theory which sounds rational is precisely the method of operation of the New World Order globalist idealism – *"Woe to those who hide deep from the Lord their counsel, whose deeds are in the dark, and who say, who sees us? who knows us? You turn things upside down!"* Isaiah 29:15-16.

Another issue which the left brought up was the fact that President Bush's salary was doubled from that of Mr.Clinton's, a one-hundred percent increase from $200,000 to $400,000. One only has to think of the ruckus some conservatives have made over small increases in minimum wage to conclude that there is weight behind some of the opposing views on the left.

With the opportunistic globalist cartels behind the American political stage and the economy, neither this President Bush nor his cabinet will venture (publicly) too far to the right. In the same manner, President Bill Clinton did not veer too much to the left in a universal integration of political powers (aka: "bi-partisanship" – an ideology which causes those who are at the extremes to incline toward the center; one which although has its pros, certainly has its cons with deadly consequences).

The left is certainly far from perfect. However, it is much more vulnerable to harsh judgement than the right, as leftists are more inclined to forgive and forget. The most recent scandal where this scenario crossed over into a parallel Biblical story was the "Monica scandal." President Clinton, though guilty of adultery, was indeed a punching bag for the extreme right. By the harsh condemnation of Clinton's sin, the right displayed exactly the sort of hypocrisy which was at the core of Christ's teaching regarding the adulteress (John 8:1-11). Furthermore, the severe abuse of the first amendment (freedom of speech / press), which the right demonstrated in their attempts to bring ruin and shame to Bill Clinton, revealed the overwhelming power of the right over much of the media. A number of "anti-Hillary" and "anti-Bill" books and articles have been published over the past decade by some conservative folk which is akin to a legion of right-wing demons attacking their prey.

The Far-Right globalists, the Religious Right, right-wing corporate magnats, right-wing revolutionists, and their aristocratic collaborators may very well get truly into gear in the next few years in their ultimate show of force by further implementing their conservative agenda aimed at the masses. This could severely "tilt the scales of justice" in this country.

THE "WAR ON DRUGS"

If the "war on terrorism" will be as the "war on drugs," we have good reason to be weary. Between the war on drugs and the Iran-Contra scandal, one was able to see that something just did not make sense. While high-caliber right-wing politicians and lawyers stepped up legislation against those possessing or selling cocaine here and particularly the cartels of Colombia, America had the infamous Iran-Contra scandal. It implicated some high-level personnel as having knowledge, at the very minimum, of military operations which actually involved cocaine trafficking. Like the Enron scandal, some used their fifth amendment right (protection from self-incrimination), vital documents were shredded, the death of a key potential witness occurred, and no one seemed to remember or know much about anything when questioned. Almost all were eventually dismissed of any wrongdoing, while some became "national heroes." If these would have been liberals, they would have been virtually crucified by the self-righteous Far-Right.

What has this quasi "war on drugs" accomplished? In short, nothing good (except for the globalists). The stymied assistance to Colombia during the 1990's, in often providing worn out and costly to repair equipment, has been to many, a mockery, in that while the Far-Right globalist collaborators aggravate the whole situation in Colombia, they profess to the American public a sincerity to fighting the drug epidemic via a "drug war." The fact that cocaine is fifty-percent cheaper today than in the early eighties is indicative of the fact that it was made economically accessible to the masses for what is to some, very obvious reasons. That supply is up in the United States is not necessarily because of Colombia, Peru, or Bolivia, but as a result of a calculated increase in demand and "more hands in the cookie jar." In other words, there has been a considerable redistribution of power in this clandestine business which arose after the fall of the Medellin and Cali cartels.

The same right-wing which began this so called war, having had its share of scandals, leaves a certain degree of skepticism in many an American's mind as to the likelihood of a deeper conspiracy. Could various "private" U.S. firms be among those fueling the demise of Colombia under misleading pretenses? The more recent $1.3 billion dollar "military aid" package to Colombia was not all it was made out to be. There were a variety of other factors which the globalists had their eyes on. Among them, were: (1) large profit potential for the American corporations that produce the "military hardware," and (2) the likelihood of increased oil ventures in Colombia.

The foreign sources (the European globalists) and their colleagues here at home, who have a vested interest in the overall decline of American culture, have had not only the motive but the finances and world-wide political clout necessary to accomplish this "transition of power." By placing "stumbling blocks" (ie: crack) among the lower echelons which promote corruption, violence, crime, aids, and prostitution, the Far-Right directly and indirectly keeps many intoxicated and often wrapped up in the legal system, thus, accelerating the New World Order (NWO) mob's immediate and long term goals: 1) To create inner-conflict and social decay in as many different ways as possible from both extremes (could this be part of the reason why those who are controlling foreign policy will not allow drugs to be legalized?); 2) By bringing this country to its knees, this mob of all mobs will create the need for drastic measures to be taken. In other words, out of the resulting economic / social destabilization and potential anarchy will "enter the dragon" (Satan, disguised as Christ and his NWO).

Little is ever said about the fact that long before Pablo Escobar's short-lived reign, it was none other than the British Oligarchy which controlled much of the drug trade as was explained in Benjamin Franklin House's *"Dope Inc. (1979)." "The New Dark Ages Conspiracy"* by Carol White followed up on this London-based international cartel. It is no surprise, then, that any high level corruption within the U.S. has direct ties to certain ultra-wealthy families in

Europe and their associates around the world. There has always been corruption within this world's governments – crooked judges, lawyers, and law enforcement who, for a variety of reasons, usually money, have not feared God, thereby perverted justice and condemned the innocent via "upside down" tactics. Isaiah 5:20: *"Woe to those who call evil good and good evil, who put darkness for light and light for darkness, who put bitter for sweet and sweet for bitter! 5:23: "..who acquit the guilty for a bribe, and deprive the innocent of his right."* See also Luke 18:2-3. (Some propose that the courts have cameras installed in the public offices of elected officials. This is big government honing in on the higher echelons. It is just a matter of time before even the wealthy and powerful are "brought to their knees" as the poor and working classes are being brought to theirs.)

That drug-warfare has been waged against certain peoples in the past is not news, but to see that the U.S. has been and is presently on the receiving end implies a much larger anathema. This can only be a product of the globalist clan who has been dismantling and corroding the U.S. and many other countries via both extremes in order to bring in their NWO. It is these serpents and their colleagues here at home who are ultimately at the core of societal breakdown, cultural demise, violence, the stripping away of rights, and the setting of traps and stumbling blocks for the masses and particularly minorities. It is these globalists who are the "top of the pyramid." Ecclesiastes 5:8 : *"If you see in a province the poor oppressed and justice and right violently taken away, do not be amazed at the matter; for the high official is watched by a higher, and there are yet higher ones over them."*

Since the actual processing of crack is done in the United States, does this implicate that other people are involved in the epidemic? Is it just a coincidence that crack is primarily found throughout the ghettos and barrios of the lower economic classes here in the U.S.? How could the cartels of Colombia have controlled the final destination of cocaine? Does it make sense that they would have targeted the lower echelons instead of the wealthy if they were targeting any class? Could it be that one of the reasons why the right is opposed to the disarmament of America is due to the fact that guns, finding their way into the black market, are simply another ploy to create havoc, chaos, and mayhem among the inner-cities? Could this shed some light as to why minorities have been killing themselves off as they have been for decades in every major U.S. city? Then that would explain the "double-jeopardy" which the inner-city is subjected to as the extreme right-wing, both here and internationally, would have a clear motive to, at least in part, clandestinely supply much of these ghettos with weapons and drugs, as they push for "10-20-Life" legislation. I am not advocating doing away with the right to bear arms, merely pointing out what is a fringe benefit to the racist Far-Right. These calculated maneuvers are simply smaller versions of what is occurring on a much grander scale: the globalists are flooding various countries with a variety of commodities such as weapons and high-technology in order to basically accomplish the same goal: debt and a weakened economy, internal strife, famine, ethnic cleansing, instability, further suppression, and chaos. These are the pre-requisites necessary for them to create the urgency for outside intervention. Then, of course, it will be they who take the credit for stepping in to save the poor wretched souls in their moments of agony and despair. This, in turn, leads to a complete take over on their part. I would not be shocked to hear Christ repeat these words to them one day: *"hypocrites! ....because you shut the kingdom of heaven against men ; for you neither enter yourselves, nor allow those who would enter to go in"* – Matthew 23:13. It just so happens to be that certain drugs have been used in recent decades, as in the past, by those who have a vital interest to derail and subjugate the masses while profiting greatly from it, a win-win scenario for the Far-Right. The globalists serve the evil empire by further exploiting the disadvantaged and vulnerable everywhere.

It may not be a coincidence then, that the Far-Right has portrayed Colombians as the ruthless worldwide bandits. It makes perfect sense: keep the spotlight on others. This end of the right, as stated before, has infiltrated even Hollywood and its stigmatizing of Colombians at large is absolute and irrefutable proof of that. It is no coincidence that the blatant as well as subliminal work of the extreme right is projected on the screen as a means to control the mindset of America. By way of legislation, the movies, and the ultra-conservative end of the media who psychologically coerces the masses through its negative imagery, these extreme right-wingers have stained the name of entire cultures of people, as the Colombian people – among various others. That there is a certain degree of racism involved here is more than clear.

It is not everyday, for instance, that Hollywood produces a movie depicting non-Hispanic white "college preps" as displaying criminal, anti-social, anti-moral, or heinous behavior. Not that they don't in real life. The irony is that many in Hollywood (and thousands of college preps) have also been quite the consumers of cocaine for decades. Movies which project Colombians as demons, drug pushers, and terrorists who want to harm mankind have severely defamed many good people. Of the minority who are involved in cocaine trafficking, I do not know of a Colombian who has ever forced anyone to snort cocaine. Did Jack Daniels or Al Capone force anyone to drink alcohol? I doubt it. Though I am not defending any of the world's drug kingpins, it is peculiar that some, who were pioneers of other enterprises, are admired and glorified. Granted, for the love of money, there have been many atrocities committed by some Colombians and certainly they will have to answer to a higher power one day, but a distinction between a minority and the majority of Colombians is long over due. Are all Italians as shady as Al Capone was? Of course not. 1 Timothy 6:9-10 applies to anyone who walks in these shoes: *"But those who desire to be rich fall into temptation, into a snare, into many senseless and hurtful desires that plunge men into ruin and destruction. For the love of money is the root of all evils; it is through this craving that some have wandered from the faith and pierced their hearts with many pangs."*

It is no shock to see the "bad side" of Colombia plastered in the media, especially on the front page of many newspapers around the world. If there is something printed of value to society which comes from Colombia, it would be quite surprising to find it on a front page. This is not a coincidence. The derogatory comments made by talk-show host David Letterman in May of 2001 in associating Andrea Noceti (Miss Colombia 2001) with a "drug mule" is just an example of the inbred mentality in the American psyche regarding Colombians in general. The Superbowl XXXVI commercials associating drug users with "terrorism" was another maneuver of the Far-Right to stir up hostility against Colombia and its people. To add insult to injury, thousands upon thousands of innocent Colombians are the ones paying a heavy price, for they have been forced to flee their land as a result of civil unrest and a crippling economy. These, however, are the "lucky ones." Many more have no option but to stay put and bear it.

Plan Colombia, the most recent agreement between the U.S. and Colombia on the issue of drugs which focuses, in part, on the fumigation and destruction of the coca plant is a catastrophic "solution" which is akin to paraquat (a chemical used by the U.S. Government in the past to exterminate that "evil plant" known as marijuana). Is marijuana extinct today? No. It continues to be grown throughout the world. Ironically, there is more homegrown (within the continental U.S.) marijuana today than ever before. Supposedly, a five year goal to eradicate the coca plant will accomplish this, and even if this were possible, it could easily grow elsewhere. There is certainly enough profit potential for this business to just be relocated to another country. This "plan" has severely affected Colombia, its indigenous people, and the ecology for the worst, while in the mean time some of those who profess to be dedicated to this war have ulterior motives behind their gentle, caring, and kind demeanor.

The demand for drugs, as many have stated before, is where the bulk of the problem lies. Thus, it is on this front that a true war on drugs lies. For decades, many politicians have tried to get world leaders to focus more on this end of the problem. This position was further exacerbated by the lose-lose scenario in the 1980's and early 1990s which left the Colombian Administrations trying to cooperate with U.S. foreign policy (ie: extraditions) while having to contend with threats and violence at home. Because regional violence and bloodshed are likely to escalate in Colombia, an incline toward a heavy-handed draconian approach is precisely what the globalists want. Many of these globalists who propose peace are really wolves dressed as sheep. They are directly and indirectly aiding Satan in his goal to spill as much innocent blood as possible in Colombia and elsewhere. These are the "peacemakers" who were prophesied to enter the global political platform prior to Christ's return. We should take note of Christ's words in John 14:27, *"Peace I leave with you; my peace I give to you; not as the world gives do I give to you."* It is worth noting that the U.S. has one-tenth of the world's population, yet consumes most of the cocaine produced in the world. In contrast, the coca-producing countries have a relatively low level of drug abuse despite the abundance of cocaine. The insatiable appetite of the American consumer has increased post the "just say no" era as the globalists wanted because there has not been a true war on drugs. We should also remember that the more we tell people they should not or cannot do something, the more they will want to. Despite many "raids" by law enforcement, illegal drugs continue to be manufactured right here in the U.S., as is methamphetamine or LSD. GHB, aka: "the date rape drug" has also reached epidemic proportions, yet the makers of this drug are not being hunted down as others are. The newest hip, hard drug, "ecstacy" which is a multi- billion dollar European industry has certainly not received the media attention that others have either.

TOBACCO, MARIJUANA, ALCOHOL, AND THE USE OF INTOXICANTS
It was God who made the tobacco plant, thus, tobacco in its rawest natural form was not "bad," but mankind who came along and made it bad by adding chemicals, processing aids, casing materials, flavoring agents, etc.- all of which may very well raise the likelihood of health complications when ingested all at once and smoked. The rationale of some corporations is that these additives are found in many foods, thus, safe. But mankind does not smoke his food, nor are there hundreds of chemicals in most fruits and vegetables. For the conservative big tobacco industry to liberally add chemicals to their tobacco, which hooks many a teenager, with no regard for possible physiological reactions which could cause serious injury in due time is a severe tort (civil wrong) – and conspiratorial. It is quite pathetic that some corporations have spent tens of millions of dollars "blowing trumpets" for all to see their ridiculous brand of charity in their TV advertisements displaying the good deeds they do. Mat-

thew 6:3-4: *"But when you give alms, do not let your right hand know what your left hand is doing, so that your alms may be in secret; and your Father who sees in secret will reward you."* According to the World Health Organization, Big Tobacco smuggles 25% of exported cigarettes into countries like Colombia and Canada in order to avoid local tariffs.

As to marijuana, the "jury is still out" with respect to its use in Biblical times. Some contend that the term "kaneh-bosm" is cannabis or calamus in the Hebrew scriptures. They claim that it was used in burnt offerings, among the priests, and as medicine for a variety of ailments. Prior to Christ's birth, however, it was used for centuries throughout Asia. It is only illegal today because of the Far-Right and its strong lobbyists who stand to lose millions if this herb is ever legalized. Between just big tobacco and the pharmaceutical industry, millions would be lost to the legalization of this herb. It is a travesty of justice to incarcerate people who cultivate, possess, or use marijuana. Only the Far-Right rationalizes spending millions of dollars to imprison people for the cultivation, possession, or consumption of this God-given plant. While many white- collar criminals, child molesters, and rapists roams the streets, numerous people convicted for cultivating or possessing marijuana are sentenced to many years in prison. Many arguments have been made against marijuana, but once again, (just for the record) tobacco and alcohol are indeed worse for society at large than this herb could ever be, and we all know Christ turned water into wine – a wine of exquisite quality at that -John 2:10. It is highly probable that Christ would condone an adult using marijuana either for medicinal purposes or as one would have a beer after a hard day's work. To some very conservative folk, Proverbs 31:6-7 may come as a bit of a shock : *"Give strong drink to him who is perishing and wine to those in bitter distress; let them drink and forget their poverty, and remember their misery no more"* – (interesting to note that in today's "politically correct" society, we condemn a homeless man for wanting a beer). 1 Timothy 5:23: *"No longer drink only water , but use a little wine for the sake of your stomach and your frequent ailments."* Christ himself came "eating and drinking" – *"For John came neither eating nor drinking and they say, 'He has a demon'; the Son of Man came eating and drinking, and they say, 'behold a glutton and a drunkard, a friend of the tax-collectors and sinners! Yet wisdom is justified by their deeds"* (Matthew 11:18-19). Using these three excerpts as a base for discerning these delicate topics should incline at least the Biblically oriented conservatives to a more lenient position. It is clear throughout the Bible that being sober and watchful is certainly recommended, but if one is to indulge, moderation is key in the consumption of alcohol – Ephesians 5:18-20 (again we see that crucial middle ground). It is also clear alcohol in excess, or anything for that matter, is not of God, that a fine line is drawn and when one has gone over it, one is subjecting himself or herself to the wiles of Satanic forces (aka: spiritual "powers and principalities").

Most likely, Christ would condemn laws which would in effect make a criminal out of someone who consumes marijuana. It could be that cannabis may actually be a most "holy" plant – all plants are holy for that matter. It has [seven] leaves and is divided into three on the left, three on the right, and a large one in the middle. It makes sense then, that most of this un-holy world's governments condemn it – and its users.

The Libertarian Party's position as to the drug epidemic is indeed the most sound and just of any party in that it is not right to incarcerate and punish a person who may actually need help. Only hard line conservative legalistic ideology rationalizes and deduces that the addicts of this world (ie: oftentimes talented ones as Robert Downey Jr) need to be dealt with by the legal system. These people are suffering from disorders which require spiritual or medical intervention, not legal. Yes, the human body is indeed the "temple of God," and it is a sin against one's own self to over-indulge. However, this sin is one which is first and foremost between that person and God, as the body which is being affected is not property of the state or any one else, but of God and that person. Perhaps legalizing some drugs is not such a bad idea after all. After prohibition, this country as a whole fared better off by legalizing alcohol than by continuing that useless war. Since this option is "too far out in left field" for many, some degree of decriminalization, amnesty, and leniency, coupled with much better rehabilitation would be much better for society, as then we would not be throwing huge stones as we have been doing at so many sinners via the established conservative legalism which is at the core of this dilemma.

Why is the long arm of the law so involved in what an adult chooses to ingest in privacy? Unless we are dealing with someone who has a severe mental deficiency which would prevent him or her from making rational decisions or someone who is endangering another, the law should not have any say. The hard line against thousands of people who consume one or another intoxicant has become a major source of revenue for many in the criminal justice / legal industry which could further explain why it is illegal to possess or consume drugs in the first place. If he or she who is overtaken in a sin against himself or herself is deemed by the more conservative crowd as being necessarily "bad," may they keep in mind the moral of the story in the parable about *"the kingdom of heaven"* in Matthew 22. Though it is not for me to say, it may very well be that God will forgive many hard drug addicts for their sins against themselves. Galatians 6:1- *"Bretheren, if a man is overtaken in a trespass, you who are spiritual should restore him in a spirit of gentleness."* Those who claim to be "righteous" should be slow to anger and fast in helping those who society has little patience with (as Christ would). By being merciful, we are just, and it is by being just, that we show faith. Though there are plenty of drug addicts who simply like getting high or escaping this world, many are either undergoing considerable internal turmoil or were victims of one or another circumstance. Thus, they are numbing psychologically devastating events which are in their past or just trying to forget their poverty and seemingly hopeless future.

This explains, in part, why there is oftentimes a totally opposite ambiance between the lower and higher echelons as to the consumption of drugs and alcohol. While many of those who are successful and "have a life" (ie: white-collar professionals) socially use cocaine or other drugs in a "partying" or "celebrating" manner, thousands who are suppressed, subjugated, and stigmatized as losers tend to abuse drugs and alcohol to forget their misery and lack of life – and the globalists knew this years ago. While these professionals pass around a tray of cocaine at a Friday night party, many in the inner city get caught up in the cycle of hard addiction. If depression and "the blues" cause some very wealthy people to end up in rehabilitation clinics and hospitals, how much more devastating it is for those who have little money, thus, few places to turn to for quality help. Since it is Satan who is ultimately behind those who auto-destruct, for the globalists and their Far-Right collaborators to "have a field day" with those who abuse hard drugs and become slaves to them, when it is some of them who also profit from the trade, is further proof of just how "down right and dirty" the extreme right can be.

In conclusion, I respectfully urge the reader to keep in mind that America's overall decline and South America's dire situation have indeed been fueled by clandestine international Far-Right policies. While the economies of South America continue to decline (thanks to the globalists), the desperation of millions of people causes many to turn to the drug trade. For this reason, if for no other, the supply of cocaine will not cease to exist. Colombia, Peru, and Bolivia have been brought to virtual ruin primarily because of one or two of the plants made by God. Another interesting point: both the U.N. and the Church are quite involved in the politics of these nations, particularly Colombia. Simon Bolivar's vision of a "liberated South America" is precisely what the Far-Right opposes. For decades, the U.N. has been a formidable player in the "war on drugs." Its involvement in this war was greatly increased following the 1987 International Conference on Drug Abuse and Illicit Trafficking which was held in Vienna (Luard, p.67).

Due to (1) the fact that governments have the capacity to regulate this industry, generate revenue, and simultaneously reduce corruption, violence, kidnappings, crime, aids, and prostitution throughout the world; (2) the severe and catastrophic breakdown of entire countries like Colombia, Peru, and Bolivia; (3) the fact that many law-enforcement officers here and all over the world are being put in harms way in vain; (4) the fact that cocaine and other hard drugs are more rampant than when this "war on drugs" began; (5) the fact that drug abusers present a spiritual or medical issue and not a legal one;

(6) the array of other drugs that are not produced by South American countries which are oftentimes produced here in the U.S. or Europe, I strongly believe we have come to a point where there is no better option than to legalize most drugs. I am not, however, advocating [for] the use of any substance, except a little wine and in various cases, cannabis / marijuana, as it is medicinal for so many adults.

SELECTED CREDITS

Blacks Law Dictionary, sixth ed. West Publishing, 1990. {"Latin" Terminology}

The Tampa Tribune, Gary Sprott, *"Judges, Lawyers Gather for Annual Red Mass,"* 1998.

The Tampa Tribune / The Associated Press, Jennifer Loven, *"Jailhouse Blues Hits New High,"* Monday, August 27, 2001.

Boston Globe, Charles M. Sennott, *"The $150 Billion 'Welfare' Recipients: U.S. Corporations: First of Three Parts,"* July 7, 1996.

U.S. News & World Report, Elise Ackerman and Margaret Loftus, *"What Money Can't Buy,"* July 12, 1999. {Ralph Nader}

Hispanic Magazine, Lupe Solis, *"Reform Critical for Latinas,"* January / February 2001.

The Tampa Tribune, Pam Noles, *"The Welfare Life: It's No Candy Store for Recipients of Aid,"* Sunday, September 3, 1995.

The Tampa Tribune / The Associated Press, Laura Meckler, *"Welfare-to-Work Call Hard to Heed,"* Tuesday, May 27, 1997.

The Associated Press, Laura Meckler, *"Welfare Changes Not Helping Poorest,"* August 22, 1999.

The Associated Press, Philip Brasher, *"State Food Stamp Rules Found Unfair,"* August 3, 1999.

International Herald Tribune, Richard W. Stevenson, *"Strong U.S. Economy Helps All But the Poorest,"* Paris, France, Thursday, January 20, 2000.

The Associated Press, Walter R. Mears, *"'Compassionate' Is Not a New Buzzword,"* June, 18, 1999.

St. Petersburg Times Parade, *"Hunger in America,"* October 29, 2000.

Newsweek Magazine, Anna Quindlen, *"Our Tired, Our Poor, Our Kids,"* March 12, 2001.

Amnesty International, New York, N.Y.. {Human Rights} www.amnestyusa.org

The Tampa Tribune, The Washington Post, *"Trip Planned To Lonely Planet Pluto,"* December 16, 2001.

Walter E. Volkomer, *"American Government,"* 7th edition. Englewood Cliffs, New Jersey: Prentice Hall, 1995. {The Reagan / Bush and Clinton Judicial Appointments, P.265}

Newswatch Magazine, *"Bill Clinton –Last Elected President of the United States?"* January-February 1997. www.newswatchmagazine.org

Alan M. Dershowitz, *"Supreme Injustice – How the High Court Hijacked Election 2000."* Oxford, New York: University Press, 2001.

Vincent Bugliosi, *"Betrayal of America."* New York: Thunder's Mouth Press / Nation Books, 2001. {The 2000 Presidential Election}

Newsweek Magazine, David A. Kaplan, *"The Secret Vote That Made Bush President,"* September 17, 2001.

Lawrence E. Walsh, *" Firewall: The Iran-Contra Conspiracy and Cover-Up."* New York: W.W. Norton & Co, 1997.

International Herald Tribune, Clifford Krauss of the New York Times, *"U.S. Involvement in Colombia: Is Another Quagmire Lying Ahead?"* Paris, France, Friday, September 1, 2000.

Knight Ridder Newspapers Report, *"Drug War Assistance Stymied Colombia,"* March 27, 1998.

Dr James Wardner, D.M.D., *"The Planned Destruction of America."* DeBary, Fl: Longwood Communications, 1994. {Multi-National Corporations, Ch 7}

Global Exchange, *"Top Ten Reasons to Oppose US Military Aid to Colombia"* {$1.3 Billion Military Aid Package to Colombia} www.globalexchange.org/colombia/topten.html

The Nation, Aram Roston, *"It's The Real Thing: MURDER – U.S. Firms Like Coca-Cola Are Implicated in Colombia's Brutality,"* September 3/10, 2001.

Dallas Morning News, Tod Robberson, *"Plan Colombia,"* February 27, 2000.

Michael Ruppert, *"Blacks were targeted for CIA Cocaine- It Can be Proven,"* January 28,1999. www.copvcia.com

The Spotlight Newspaper, Daniel Hopsinger, *"New Head-Honcho At DEA Protected Drug Smuggler,"* Volume XXVI, Number 22, May, 28, 2001. www.spotlight.org

The Spotlight Newspaper, *"Secret History of CIA Connected Drug Smuggling & Assasination Revealed by Journalist,"* Volume XXVI, Number 23, June 4, 2001 {Barry Seal Exclusive} www.spotlight.org

Latino Internacional, *"Colombianos Indignados Por Commentarios Sobre Su*

Reina de Belleza" / "Colombians Indignant as to Comments Made of the Reigning Beauty Queen," Vol. 09, No.31, Mayo 17, 2001 / May 17, 2001.

Fox Television Network, Superbowl XXXVI, Sunday, February 3, 2002. {Anti-Colombian Commercials}

Gabriel Garcia Marquez, *"News of a Kidnapping."* New York: A Borzoi Book by Alfred A. Knopf, Inc., 1997. {Pablo Escobar}

American Banner, Doug Yurchy, *"Marijuana...What They Forgot to Tell You About Pot,"* Vol 3, Ed 16, Spt / Oct 1996.

Chris Bennet, *"Kaneh Bosm: The Hidden Story of Cannabis in the Old Testament,"* June 1996. www.hempbc.com/magazine/mayjune96/kanehbosm.html

People Magazine, *"Cover Story: Show Stopper,"* March 12, 2001 {Matthew Perry – "Vicodin"}

Time Magazine, Patti Davis, *"Dope: A Love Story,"* May 7, 2001. {Robert Downey Jr.}

R. J. Reynolds Tobacco Company, *"Cigarette Ingredients,"* Released April, 13, 1994.

The Nation, Mark Shapiro, *"Big Tobacco,"* May 6, 2002

James Adams, *"The Financing of Terror."* New York: Simon & Schuster, 1986. {The Narc-Farc Connection,Ch.9}

The Associated Press, Arthur Max, *"Liberal? Dutch Say They're Just Sensible,"* Sunday, May 27, 2001. {Legalization of Drugs}

Common Sense for Drug Policy, Kevin B. Zeese, President (2001) www.csdp.org; Info@csdp.org

Evan Luard, *"The United Nations: How it Works and What it Does,"* New York: St. Martin's Press, 1994.

CHAPTER FOUR

THE PROTESTANT MOVEMENT
AND THE ROMAN TIME-CLOCK

The Reformation, which began in the sixteenth century, brought with it a heightened awareness with regard to the Church's fallacies. The masses now had a window of opportunity to separate themselves from engaging in many of the erroneous traditions and beliefs of the Church as the Bible instructed the Christian to do. A byproduct of this was a deep thirst for the word and what it really has to say. The Reformation, then, being the birthplace of Protestantism, is what gives rise to this chapter which is anti-apostate at its core. Its message should cause those who "have an ear" (thus, hear the spirit of God) to question the Church and the coming unification with her "daughters" (the Protestant denominations) in what will culminate into the new "politically correct," yet false church of the last days. We should keep in mind that Protestantism was basically an attempt to re-establish exactly what the first "Christian Church" had taught via a new doctrine which was merely the completion of the old. For every major law which God set forth when Moses received the Ten Commandments, the only words in the Bible written by God himself, it has been of primary importance for the adversary, Satan, to mimic, copycat, alter, and/or destroy. This, then, is the root of the variety of false gods and idolatry which are of primary use to the evil empire (a severe distortion of the second commandment). Satan also created a "new world" timeframe which would detour masses of humanity from God's time-clock as the prophet Daniel predicted in Daniel 7: 25.

Though mankind does not have all the answers to the complexity of this ongoing battle between spiritual powers and principalities, it is for those who hear the messages, to question their authority, analyze the data, make a distinction between the two, and decide which one to follow. Should one follow that which was man made, or that which was written directly by the hand of the One True God?

The greatest flaw of tomorrow's Protestant movement will be its tendency to mend any broken ties with the new-age Roman Catholic Church, thus, eventually including other deities which the Church now recognizes. This will be as a "mark" which Satan will place upon those who accept the new apostate "Christian" philosophy. The second greatest weakness of the Protestant movement is its continued adherence to the Roman time-clock. In Exodus 12:2, God says, *"This month shall be to you as the beginning of months; it shall be as the first month of the year for you"* (Exodus 13:4). So, it is a fact that God gave the Israelites a distinct calendar (the only calendar Christ adhered to) to observe and hold fast to until the last day. Numbers 9:2, *"Let the people of Israel keep the Passover at its appointed time."* The fact that some Protestant leaders, as Martin Luther, were Jew haters helps explain why the Protestant movement was not completely liberated from the over-riding influence of the Vatican and its time-clock. The Bible speaks of a beast which will eventually "mark" its followers in some fashion with that infamous "six- six-six."

Likewise, God will "seal" or mark his flock – those who do not adhere to the inclusion of other gods, follow the apostate Church's political precepts, and keep the eleven commandments (includes Christ's commandment to "love one another"). This mark, then, is a war – on a spiritual dimension – for the hearts and minds of people. Some will accept a surface only brand of Christianity, believing that since it appears to be "right," it is.

Since the book of Revelations was written to a great extent in code (ie: beast, harlot, horse) to preserve it for the last days, it makes perfect sense to reason that the mark on the *"right hand or on the forehead"* (Rev.13:16) is symbolic and not literal, as many denominations and congregations teach (that the beastly-big-brother-government will force the masses to have a micro-chip surgically implanted in one's right hand or forehead). This is exactly what the conspirators want the masses to believe, as it is the apostate movement who will promote a literal meaning, precisely as Satan would have it interpreted – to fool even the wise. It is critical to keep in mind that this new world government / "new secular order" will ultimately be separatist, not inclusive; hence, it will mark many people, not all people. Neither in Exodus 13:16, nor in Deuteronomy 6:8 does it refer to some sort of object implanted into the person by God. Therefore, why would the master copycat (Satan) not do as usual and do the opposite of what God does? In Philippians 3:17 Paul instructs the saints at Philippi to *"mark those who so live as you have an example in us."* This does not mean in some literal sense. The mark, then, is not a tangible one – but a spiritual one. It is one which has to do with God's emphatic exclusion of other deities and the Anti-Christ's political precepts, commandments (or interpretation of), mandates and statutes. The ideology of this evil government will not only be associated with the Far-Right, but it will mark those who accept it on the [right] hand. It is no coincidence that it is the right hand which is explicitly mentioned and not the left. If the micro-chip theory had logic, then it would not matter if the mark were placed on the left hand. Hence, Satan wants to mark his people by placing all deities "under one Roman umbrella"- in total objection to God's ways. If one does not believe in a God, he too will fall under this umbrella. This is the manner in which Satan marks those who unfortunately fail to make that critical distinction between that which is of this wicked world and what is of a higher order. The primary reason why so many will not make this distinction is as a result of the apathy and complacency that is indeed very common these days. This lends itself to a new-age inclusion of other gods and a new spiritual correctness. Since this mark {#666}will have a connection to the Revived Roman Empire, it will have a direct link to the new age Church and its religious "inclusiveness," political ideology, mandates, customs, beliefs, and ordinances. The mark of the beast will have direct correlation to the adherence of Rome's "all deities welcome" edict, its holidays, and consequential denouncement of God's true holy days as well. Hence, those who are "sealed" by God will denounce the embracing of any other gods or goddesses and adhere to the same timetable Christ kept.

By completely ignoring the festivals of Leviticus 23 and not disengaging from the man-made holidays spoken of in chapter one (Sunday, the official day of rest; Christmas & Easter, both national / legal holidays) the "protest" of Rome was then, as it is today, simply a limited protest. This fact makes the conflicts between Protestants and Catholics (ie: "Sunday, Bloody Sunday") that much more of a pity. The August,1998 bombing in Omagh, Ireland by Catholic guerrillas which left 29 people dead leaves no doubt that religious wars and the terrorism which fuels them will serve to bring about a New World Order. Terrorists in Europe may not receive the international attention which other groups do, but they are well organized and just as volatile. Factoid: America spends more money securing its embassy in Athens, Greece, than on any other embassy in the world. This is due to the killing of Americans by the "N17."

The issue of time was a critical one in the Old Testament, and to assume that Christ manipulated in the least his Father's time-clock is preposterous. Throughout the New Testament, Christ emphatically reiterates over and over again that he does nothing on his own accord. And nowhere in the Bible is there support for the changing of his holy days or of his Hebrew time-clock. Quite to the contrary, as a Jew, Christ was under the Hebrew clock which is synonymous with true Christianity. With all due respect to many fine "Sunday folk" and Roman holiday enthusiasts, if one really wants to claim to be a true "Christian," paying a bit of attention to what is to many a seemingly insignificant issue, is of great importance. It was an issue of such magnitude, God included it among the Ten Commandments given to Moses at Mt Sinai – (again, the 4th commandment).

Another weakness Protestantism has is its major divisions and conflicts within the various denominations. Within it are a vast array of differences as to how to do this or how to do that, how to interpret this excerpt or that passage. That lack of unity is of great value to the Revived Roman Empire and to the rise of apostasy. It allows Rome to easily sway and convince many through "upside down logic" to go with the new-age program. Ironically, it will be Rome who finally brings the Protestant Churches back in line. Christians the world over should honor the many "heretics" which the Church has martyred and persecuted over the centuries, liberals as well as conservatives. It is also to them that much gratitude is owed, as they have paid with their lives often attempting to bring about a more Biblically-based Christianity. Since the Church kept the masses in the dark for so long with respect to the Bible, when the word spread about, it allowed people to "gather their notes and compare." This gave rise to the various other "daughters" which branched out with their interpretations of doctrine, much of it right on target. Many fine Protestant people of conservative ideology have realized that the conservatism of the Church is not righteous conservatism but racist and suppressive conservatism. It holds to compassion while furthering the mandates of old, the domination of the masses, and the political ideology which is very much alive in today's new age right-wing. Too bad there are not more righteous conservatives like them.

From Protestants, moderates, leftists, and liberal clergy / theologians has come a wave of efforts to sway from some of the traditional views of the Church. Those who have opposed Mother Rome's interpretation of scripture, rhetoric, and the more conservative view which the Church professes have played a key role in shaking up the stereotype of a conservative Messiah. However, they have at times severely over-compensated or have incorporated ideals which are blasphemous – such as a gay Christ or a crucified woman in place of Christ – both of these arising out of the extreme left. Then there is the "racist Christ" of the KKK – the Far-Right. It is a disgrace to see the venom of racism within many churches today, as they are not immune from the wiles of Satan. Various Protestants continue to adhere to the notion that Christ was white as they have their racist overtones which remain from Rome's teachings. It is peculiar to see the remnant of yesterday's segregation of minorities within some Protestant churches today. Fact is, many Protestant churches began as racist organizations who only relatively recently have included minorities – a few, superficially at that. Some still adhere to an underlying "us and them" protocol because they remain daughters of the Church's conservative and dominating tendencies. Fundamentally, many denominations to this day remain inclined toward the right anyway – where the Church and its time-clock are and will remain.

It is a fact that for the last three to four hundred years, The Bible has been abused by many to justify the savage, brutal, and barbaric treatment of slaves (Reader's Digest, pp. 344-345). Perhaps this sheds some light as to why mainline churches have displayed "double standards" with regard to the plight of the suffering people of Afghanistan in the past (Bork, p. 91).

SELECTED CREDITS

U.S. News & World Report, Thomas K. Grose, *"Real IRA: Really Terrorists,"* May 28, 2001.

James Adams, *"The Financing of Terror."* New York: Simon & Schuster, 1986. {The IRA Mafia, Ch.7}

BBC News, Edward Stourton, *"Europe / Justice: A Greek Tragedy, N17,"* December, 2000. www.news.bbc.co.uk/hi/english/audiovideo/programm.../ 1205893.st {American Embassy in Athens, Greece}

Reader's Digest, *"The Bible through the Ages."* Pleasantville, New York, 1996.

Robert H. Bork, *"Slouching towards Gomorrah."* New York: Regan Books, 1996.

CHAPTER FIVE

THE COMING APOSTATE CHURCH AND RIGHT-WING THEOLOGY

Where will that last day apostate Christian Church rise from? It will rise from the new and revived right-wing dominated, yet somewhat leftist, "All-Inclusive-Church" and those who will accept her invitation to come together as one. We can see the trend in the GOP and the Religious Right to blend in with the end-time Catholic Church. America and the world should keep a very close eye on the likely endorsement of "Christianity" by any government, for that will be the opportunity Satan has been awaiting to one day claim he is the Christ.

Jesus Christ made it very clear that the state and God were to be kept separate, that one is to render to Rome what is Rome's and to God what is God's. Hence, a distinction which was to be throughout time, for Rome was, is, and will be exclusively of this world (Matthew 22:21). Rome's brand of hardened right-wing justice was portrayed as cold-hearted and merciless even by Christ. Thus, we would do well to steer clear of it. Luke 12:57-59: *"And why do you not judge for yourselves what is right? As you go with your accuser to the magistrate, make an effort to settle with him on the way, lest he drag you to the judge and the judge hand you over to the officer and the officer put you in prison. I tell you, you will never get out till you have paid the last copper."* Out of the coming intermingling between big government, the legal system, and "organized religion" will arise the apostate right-wing Christian Church. It is also becoming more common to see intermingling between people of even conflicting religious beliefs. Though this comradeship is to be applauded, when it goes overboard, as prophesied, the outcome will be disastrous for many. In a glorious show of unification, one day, all faiths will be integrated by a world government. This will cause God's true people, or those who "do not go with the flow," to eventually be persecuted via a "New World Constitution" which will not provide the great freedom of religion America has today. It is very critical to observe that it will be an "upside down" logic used to pervert the masses into going with the flow of the apostasy. Therefore, those who oppose this, will be hated as prophesied. Among the tactics which will be used lies the fact that the true people of God, by being portrayed as "separatists," will be deemed evil, thus, not "fitting in with the crowd" (the unification of religions). We should never forget that Jesus Christ himself was a "separatist." Matthew 13:30, *"..at harvest time, I will tell the reapers, gather up the weeds first and bind them in bundles to be burned, but gather the wheat into my barn."* Luke 6:22, *"Blessed are you when men hate you, and when they exclude you and revile you, and cast out your name as evil on account of the Son of man!"*

Various prophetic books in both the Old and New Testaments refer to a "falling away" which will cause even some of the most educated to fall into Satan's trap as chapter 24 of Matthew describes – *"to fool even the elect."* What does this delicate and politically charged chapter reveal? Lets observe closer a few key points: the *"hardness of the heart"* which when *"wickedness is multiplied"* and as verse 10 explains, *"...many will fall away and betray one another, and hate one another"* – this is absolutely and without question whatsoever, directly related to the Far-Right which is after all the ideology which is paramount when *"men's love will grow cold"* (verse12). We are indeed at the threshold of this rigid and callous society which is self-absorbed, self-righteous, and self-centered.

Note: There are some fine conservative theologians who clearly do not fall into the following category, therefore, this is not a generalization.

The Religious Right and various Protestant partners have played a key role in the conservative portrayal and interpretation of The Father, Christ, and the scriptures. Therefore, it is no surprise that it will be the right which predominates and consequently makes every attempt to legislate for its ethical positions. It is worth noting that many of the popular contemporary American preachers are curiously devout republicans who profess a conservative political ideology not-too-distant in overall policy from the traditional Church. Without criticizing the act of tithing, it is no surprise that so many "theologians" use and abuse the following excepts from Malachi 3:7-8: *"From the days of your fathers you have turned aside from my statutes and have not kept them. Return to me and I will return to you, says the Lord of hosts. But you say, 'How shall we return?' Will man rob God? Yet you are robbing me. But you say, 'How are we robbing thee?' In your tithes and offering's."* Many conservative preachers ask and almost demand a considerable amount of money on a very frequent basis for the sake of the ministry and for their "religious packages" revealing "God's truth" to those who have good money to pay for it. I guess if you are poor, you do not deserve to hear the "word of God." It is these conservative false prophets who propose generous tithing to the ministry while emphatically pushing for welfare reform legislation which takes the bread out of the mouths of babes. It is interesting how these conservatives sometimes promote being "liberal" and "generous." I wonder what Christ thinks of this? It is these wise and crafty serpents who "blow trumpets" and propagandize their good works only to be seen by men. Their "conservative Christian ministries" are oftentimes multi-million dollar political enterprises under the guise of theological and humanitarian entities which abuse the scriptures for their own profit. Within many of the modern day churches, one can belong to the "layman's circle" for a certain pledge while others in higher income brackets can buy into the "big-man's circle" for some ridiculous and astronomical "love gift" which will supposedly enlighten the tither's spiritual path that much more. With gadgets such as diplomas, charms, pamphlets, peanuts, or prayer cloths to offer the public for their donation, many are the target of this multi-million dollar conservative industry. Through "spiritual marathons" and "prophecy seminars," which are frequently a means of brainwashing thousands of people into opening their pocketbook and donating to "God's work," the apostasy of Christianity is on the rise.

With the excuse that it is God's calling to raise large sums of money for "the ministry," many, not knowing how to decipher between the real and the fake prophet, have been deceived into giving over and over again, even to the point of giving everything one owns over to "the Lord." It is without question that if a preacher is using his position of trust to deceive folks into purchasing "Godly-packages" or giving "love-gifts" in order to get rich, this is a prime example of a false prophet. These are among the false and profit oriented ministries that are among the vipers who prey on the ignorance, weakness, and even desperation of others (ie: those seeking to be healed). In the New Testament it says much about last day prophets in sheep's clothing and that we would recognize them by their "fruits." If the "ministry" and the Bible are in conflict, that should be a red flag.

Another example that someone is over-stepping their call to serve God is he or she who predicts the day of Christ's return. Even Christ did not know when he would be sent back again. Therefore, how can any of us sinners know? Incidentally, there are false teachers who come from all races: as black, brown, white, yellow, and red men-just like the fact that there are good men of all colors and religions (certainly there are many good people of non-Jewish / non-Christian beliefs). The Old Testament thoroughly explains how God reacted with fury against those who claimed to be Jews, yet were false, pagan, and idolatrous. King Herod, who was a "Roman-Jew" may very well have fit the mold. Acts 13:6, for instance, explains of a "Jewish false prophet." We need to discern between someone who sells information or literature at reasonable prices to cover overhead and live modestly, as it is with the support of the congregation that they oftentimes live on, and those capitalizing on the mass-marketing of their wolverine and despicable tactics. There are both "Jews" and "Christians" who have been making a mint this way, many of which are indeed staunch right-wingers.

Public displays of their "self-righteous religion" (ie: school prayer) are just another example of their intrusiveness to mold the masses into one Christian religion, the last day "apostate religion." This religion blends with all others because it embraces the false version or false interpretation of the Ten Commandments. The integration of their "Christ" into public schools is indeed another example of the right imposing their dogma on everyone else. To encourage the young to pray is good; for the state to endorse any religious activity in a public setting is not. Though I am a proponent of the (Biblical) Ten Commandments, I am watchful of cases where they are falsely interpreted and shoved into the public domain. The secular establishment has not exactly been the forum for Biblical doctrine. To blend true Christianity with this "Darwinian" entity is akin to mixing oil and water, hence the need to bring Catholics, Protestants, and others under one umbrella, or an all-inclusive Christianity which does not question some of the most fundamental precepts of the Bible.

ABORTION

It is clear that we are moving into a delicate period with respect to reproductive laws, as it is highly probable that there will be, as in other highly controversial topics, a gradual intrusion from the Far-Right. At the time of this writing, the state of Virginia, a heavyweight for conservatism, is moving in this direction.

The Far-Right's staunch anti-abortion position is another hot political issue of the day which will be a high point of interest in the immediate future. The legal conflicts arising out of the Church's mergers with some hospitals and the subsequent banning of abortions is sure to continue being a struggle between the right and the part of the left which is not yet under Roman rule. Among the vast right-wing's political and religious agenda is to come together to ban the right for women to choose. While this happens, many republicans dare claim they are [for] women and small government... interesting.

Liberals want to minimize abortions. Because they are against it, they condone family planning which reduces the need for reproductive medical care, in turn, actually preventing abortions. (I am not advocating [for] the distribution of condoms in public high schools.

Since America's teenage birthrate is the highest in the developed world, society may do well in fully addressing the factors which are condoning a promiscuous culture.)

Because all life is precious, females (and the males involved) should avoid unwanted pregnancies. Deuteronomy 30;19: *"Therefore choose life."* This mandate, however, should not be enforced by any government of this world. Once again, true "Christians" should not force their views on others. This would be no different than the brutal inquisitions. Since it is highly probable that one day in the not-too-distant future Roe v. Wade (1973 – Texas) could be overturned by the extreme right political and religious machine, society will be throwing many a stone at women who abort, for then the illegal act of aborting one's own fetus will become a crime punishable by fines, incarceration, or perhaps even death. After all, if one is found guilty of first degree murder, which is what a woman could theoretically be charged with, does he or she not get life in prison or a death sentence?

The bottom line is that it is primarily anger which fuels the motive to actually murder another human being – a human emotion which is usually void when a woman chooses to abort. It is a fact that one of the commandments is "though shall not murder / kill" – but what if that killing is of a merciful origin as are many abortions, and of course, euthanasia?

The Bible says "there is a time for everything" – or in other words a time to do what may be to some as a conflict of (religious) interest – as in, to kill –see Ecclesiastes 3:1-8. Sometimes in life, extreme circumstances do arise which allow for extreme measures to be taken. In fact, many women are driven to abort in order to avoid raising a child in severe poverty or giving him or her up to the establishment of today where the child may remain throughout its first 18 years of life being re-transplanted every few years to a new set of "parents." For many women then, it is actually a partly humane act. Akin to abortion was the desperate situation of those Jews at Massada – where one was faced with a choice to live as an animal or die with what little dignity was left, thus, taking the glory away from Rome / Satan. Will God hold this suicide pact against them?

Contrary to popular belief, the ultra-conservative crowd's belief: The Bible does not support the enactment of such laws or worse, castigating women for aborting their fetus. The philosophy of Ecclesiastes 4:1-3 may be disturbing to some: *"Again, I saw all the oppressions that are practiced under the sun. And behold the tears of the oppressed and they had no one to comfort them! On the side of their oppressors there was power and there was no one to comfort them. And I thought the dead who are already dead more fortunate than the living who are still alive; but better than both is he who has not yet been, and has not seen the evil deeds that are done under the sun."* Thus, at times, it may be better to not ever have existed in this evil world. This excerpt may cause the Far-Right a bit of frustration in Biblically justifying the reversal of Roe v. Wade. The Church and its Religious Right allies hold the same view: that the Church should legislate morality or in other words that the government endorse their interpretation of Christianity – that is a daunting idea. This decision is ultimately one between a woman, the man involved, and their God only. It is a critical decision that when big government muscles in on in the name of "righteousness," we go from a democracy to a theocracy. When such personal and private issues move from the bedroom to the courtroom, Church becomes State via a bully government who will profess that "it's for your own good"- a very common position these days for the enactment of laws restricting our freedom. What just stuns me is how many right-wingers are supposedly [for] minimizing big government because it is overly intrusive into the private lives of the people, yet somehow they rationalize enacting laws which order a woman to have a child, regardless of her right over her own body.

Just what are the "weightier issues" to ponder? 1) A woman's reproductive and medical care should be respected by the massive right (religious and political) as it is that woman's right over that which pertains to God first and to her second (she can take it up with her deity, if she believes in one), third to the male involved and ninety-ninth to all others concerned; 2) While child and juvenile foster-care and adoption is in crisis as it is at present time, due in large part, ironically, to the Far-Right's social "reforms," the argument for adoption is a weak one, if one at all. (Incidentally, it is more probable that modest liberals would adopt a child, even more-so, one not of their race, culture, or background); 3) It is foolish to think that by outlawing abortion, it would drastically decrease; 4) The hard line conservatives are without doubt "throwing the first stone" at a sinner when they are oftentimes among the "puritans" (aka: hypocrites) Christ strongly differed with.

It is not only here in the U.S. where allowing for birth-control, which is ultimately rooted in fairness, is a sensible approach to limiting unwanted births. Similar struggles between Church and State on these most delicate topics are unfolding everywhere, as has been the case in some South American countries in recent times. (As to terrorists who bomb abortion clinics or threaten to kill doctors or nurses, it seems this brand of terrorism is not exactly repugnant to some conservatives.)

STEM CELL RESEARCH
Though some might propose that the government should harvest embryos – a frightening thought, stem cell research certainly has a promising side which could eventually lead to miracles for some.

~HEY LUCIFER~
Yours are the battles in our midst,
The suffering of nations,
The despair of our elders,
The hatred between men,
The agony of women,
The tears of children,
The trials we experience,
The tribulations we encounter,
The horrors at our footsteps,
The violence in our souls,
The pain in our hearts,
The wickedness in our minds,
The powers we don't see,
The principalities we don't recognize,

The stumbling blocks we trip over,
The loneliness we feel,
The nightmares we dream,
The demons that ravage us,
The moments we wish we were never born.

L. F. G.

EUTHANASIA AND CAPITAL PUNISHMENT

It is amazing to see the ultra-conservatives promote capital punishment, yet they condemn the freedom of choice and euthanasia. Does
a person on their "death bed" not deserve the right to "throw in the
towel" and call it quits? If the Bible suggests one commit suicide if
he is a glutton (Proverbs 23:2), why would one find it immoral to
allow a person who is deathly ill to say their last goodbye with dignity instead of living in horrific conditions and oftentimes in great
pain? The gall of the Far-Right to prevent a terminally ill person
from dying in peace is absolutely mind-boggling. Why can't they
just live and let die? Again, how can republicans claim they are for
the reduction of big government when it is the legal system which
has the power to play God in mandating that a very ill person cannot
just "pull the plug?" The mentally sound parent of a deathly ill child
should have complete power over the length of time the child remains suffering without further worry over a potential charge of
murder or legal problems (ie: Dr. Kevorkian's conviction). I am not
necessarily pro-suicide, however, at times this is the only humane
recourse.

The Catholic Church's anti-death penalty position may be its most
Biblically- paralleled belief. Historically, it has been extremely pro-
death penalty. This too, may be among the few remaining issues for
the GOP to grapple with in light of the Church's standing today on
killing a criminal. If even one person is wrongly executed, that is
enough to do away with this vengeful rightist law. Does capital punishment not fall under the category of the "taking of a life?" Do some
criminals not deserve the opportunity to repent and possibly recompense society? If a mentally sound prisoner wants to commit suicide,

that is another story – he or she should be given the means to. What if the defendant has serious mental illness ("disorders" which may be the result of demonic possession)? If the crime was so heinous, he or she will be in jail until death anyway. To many this fate is worse than dying by lethal injection. Therefore, if it is from a punishment standpoint, life in prison seems plenty adequate. If the fact that Christ did not allow the adulteress to be stoned to death, as was customary, is not enough to convince them that the death penalty was abolished by Christ, perhaps they are not lending an ear to the essence of his actions and parables. Matthew 5:38-42 explains verbatim that the old law of *"an eye for an eye"* is as of then, obsolete. I realize this is not always feasible. However, we know the infamous words: *"Vengeance is mine, says the Lord"* (Romans 12:19). Christ basically directs his flock to actually *"love your enemy."* Though this may seem impossible, the morale of the story is "you who follow me, must go the extra mile." If the followers react as the masses, how then are they to be distinguished? We are under his mandate to rise above the condemnation which is all too common a characteristic of the Far-Right. In other words, we must strive, as is possible, to be more than the average person.

SELECTED NOTES

Newsweek Magazine, *"The Pope: Come Unto Me?"* June 4, 2001. {The Church Welcomes Protestants, Others}

The Tampa Tribune, Ronnie Blair, *"Views Differ on 'In God We Trust,'"* Sunday, September 9, 2001.

Terry Eastland, Editor, *"Religious Liberty in the Supreme Court, The Cases That Define the Debate Over Church and State."* Washington D.C.: Ethics and Public Policy Center, 1993.

The Tampa Tribune, Ben Feller, *"Panel OK's School Prayer,"* Friday, April 6, 2001.

The Tampa / Chicago Tribune – Nation / World, *"Top Alabama Justice's Action On Ten Commandments Monumental,"* Sunday August 19, 2001.

"Ten Commandments Defense Act Ammendment Passes Overwhelmingly," June 17, 1999. www.house.gov/aderholt/10one.html

United Synagogues of Conservative Judaism Position Papers, *"Posting the 10 Commandments in Public Schools,"* June 18, 1999. www.uscj.org.y (USCJ opposes)

Church & State, *"Preachers, Politics, and Campaign,"* Vol. 53 No.8, September 2000. {The "Christian" Religious-Right}

The Arab-American Mirror, *"The American Judeo-Christian Club and the Politics of Exclusion,"* New York, 1998. www.geocities.com/aamirror/exclude.htm

Planned Parenthood, Fact Sheet, *"Opposing Dangerous Hospital Mergers,"* 2001.

El Tiempo, *"Iglesia Catolica rechaza fallo de la Corte sobre aborto"* / *"Catholic Church rejects error of Court on abortion,"* Bogota, Colombia, Viernes 22 de junio de 2001 / Friday, June 22, 2001.

The Associated Press, Paul Sloca, *"Pope's Plea Saves Death Row Inmate,"* Friday, January 29,1999.

The Tampa Tribune, Sam Howe Verhovek of The New York Times, *"Ashcroft Stamps Out Oregon's Assisted Suicide,"* November 7, 2001.

CHAPTER SIX

PART 1

GOD AND CHRIST IN THE MIDST OF THE OLD AND NEW TESTAMENTS

It has been said by some that the Hebrew menorah detailed in Exodus 25:31 has profound mystery, and I am of the opinion that this is true. For me, the "center" candle is symbolic of God and Christ. It was actually Moses who built the first "golden lampstand" – a [seven] candle Menorah as explained in Exodus 25:31-38. In light of the political overtone of this book bringing to light the fallacies of the Far-Right in particular, without defending the Far-Left in the least, the middle-ground may also be representative of God and Christ's perfect balance, of their impeccable justice, and of them being "in the midst," yet surrounded by perfect equilibrium at both sides. From the very beginning of the entire Bible, the Old Testament, we can see that in Genesis 2:9 the tree of life is in the midst of the garden. This divine tree was placed in the middle, not to the right or to the left. A further look into this seemingly insignificant observation reveals that throughout the scriptures, the throne of God, true righteousness, and his dwelling place are primarily "centrist." The following are the most pertinent Biblical excerpts which completely support this conclusion:

   In Exodus 3:2, the angel of God appears from the midst of
   a burning bush.
   In Exodus 24:16, God calls out to Moses from the midst

of the cloud.

In Joshua 1:7, as in 23:6, we see that God is explaining that the Mosaic law was indeed centrist and that one should be careful to not sway to either left or right.

In 1 Kings 3:8, thy servant is in the midst of thy people.

In 2 Kings 22:2, we notice Josiah, a King of Jerusalem for thirty-one years, neither turned to the right or left – this is what was right in the eyes of God.

In 2 Chronicles 18:18, we see that all of the host of heaven are at both sides, not only on the right, but the left as well.

In Ezekiel 43:9, God will dwell in the midst of his people if they will give up their wicked ways.

In Ezekiel 48:8, and 48:21, God clearly portrays the sanctuary of the temple to be in the middle.

In Proverbs 4:26-27, we see an astounding warning that most emphatically warrants attention – to lean to either the left or right can be evil.

In Hosea, The "Holy One" is in the midst.

In Joel 2:27, God asserts his position as being in the midst of Israel.

In Zephaniah 3:15 and 3:17, God is in the midst.

In Zechariah 8:3, God returns to Zion and dwells in the midst.

In Matthew 18:20, Christ continues the tradition by explaining that he is in the midst.

In Mark 15:27, Christ is crucified between two robbers.

In Hebrews 9:15, Christ is the (mediator) of a new covenant.

In Revelations 1:13, the prophetic message of Christ is amidst seven lamp-stands.

In Revelations 4:6, the throne of God and the equilibrium on each side are highlighted.

In Revelations 7:17, the Lamb (Christ) is in the midst as the shepherd.

It may not be surprising, then, that the whole of God is indeed a perfect blend of right and left.

PART 2

EVIL IN THE MIDST AND THE ANTI-CHRIST

As has been for millennia, the adversary (Satan) and his crew are presently, and will continue to be, a masquerading entity which appear as sheep but are actually wolves. In order to appear truly Godly, Satan must use a scheme which mimics that of God and Christ, and therefore, it is not a shock that the Genesis account which explains where in the garden the tree of life is, also shows a counterpart at the very same location. The other tree, the tree of knowledge of good and evil is right there from the start. Since it is a fact that mankind has become much more knowledgeable in just the last century in every sense, including spiritually, it is important to realize that this knowledge of good and evil requires God's counterpart to turn up the heat on mankind while there is time. With that said, he needs to take more calculating and cunning moves in order to sway as many as possible toward deception. He will then obviously be forced to project a very Christ-like image since it is Jesus Christ of "the order of Melchizedek" to whom the torch has been passed to in the heavens, and it is he who is the true Lion of the Tribe of Judah (Psalm 110:4 and Hebrews 7).

A centrist "politically correct" position, a humane and inclusive demeanor, and a compassionate heart will be among the "publicly outward appearances" of this Anti-Christ and needless to say of his collaborators who precede him, from both extremes. Throughout the

Old Testament, there is example after example of how Satan caused many to worship foreign gods, to break their pact with God Almighty, to commit spiritual adultery, and violate the very first commandment of Exodus 20. His constant intrusive presence caused God to smite a barrage of peoples time and again. In Jeremiah 50:8, the midst of Babylon is where the center for satanic activity was, so God sent his condemnation and directed his "flock" to flee. The book of Job reveals that Satan was right there in the midst trying his best to do whatever he could to bring Job to curse God. We should not forget that this world has been so much in Satan's power that even Christ was proposed a "settlement" by him which is vividly explained in the New Testament – again, evil is right in the midst (Luke 4:1-8).

Prophetically, there has been a great deal of attention given by people around the world and by the scriptures themselves which reveal that Satan, in his most elaborate ploy ever, will incarnate into the infamous Anti-Christ. In this endeavor, he will be innately inclined to alter traditional world-wide political and religious power centers, hence, the Catholic Church itself. It will be quite imperative to make the ways of old appear as un- Godly thus warranting his intervention.

A superficially centrist and inclusive, but right-wing dominated "New World Order" is at our doorstep; it is where we have been heading for some time now. Many politicians have used this term in their addresses to the people of the United States and the United Nations.

Does the present aura of many bi-partisan / centrist views within the American political landscape have a correlation to the coming centrist Anti-Christ? Is bi-partisanship attempting to bring a "oneness" to the U.S. political stage in order to open another door which will be the beginning of the end? Is mankind being politically "marinated" before entering the New World Order "oven?" Could it be that this is the Revived Roman Empire's grand conspiracy which is preparing the masses for the Anti-Christ's appearance on the world's political stage? Does this explain why it is a "vast right-wing conspiracy" which encompasses much of the left into its modern day diabolic framework using high technology as a means to reach total domination? Is it a coincidence that the universal computer format used today is called "Times New Roman?" Could this be the vile-last- day-world-government prophesied for so long? Will Satan arise out of this forum when mankind has reached a pivotal and critical global circumstance (ie: an international financial collapse) which no mortal human can fix?

One point needs to be clarified before proceeding. Since many of those who follow Christ clearly understand and believe that this evil world will have a dramatic ending, it is imperative to keep in mind that those who truly echo Biblical prophecy / eschatology are not "doomsayers." Quite the opposite, they are bringing to the fore-front the "good news" that in due time this wicked world will be invaded by celestial forces which will do away with the temporary reign of Satan in order to establish a truly righteous and eternal world government under the leadership of Thee Jesus Christ. This is the good news which will come immediately after the "great day of the Lord": *"The great day of the Lord is near, near and hastening fast; the sound of the day of the Lord is bitter, the mighty man cries aloud there. A day of wrath is that day, a day of distress and anguish, a day of ruin and devastation, a day of darkness and gloom, a day of clouds and thick darkness, a day of trumpet blast and battle cry against the fortified cities and against the lofty battlements"* (Zephaniah 1:14-16). Jesus Christ: *"Do not think that I have come to bring peace on earth; I have not come to bring peace, but a sword"* - Matthew 10:34.

To delve into potential answers to these monumental questions, it is only prudent to look at what the scriptures say and then discern them as they apply to the virtually border-less world of today. There are various books in both the Old and New Testaments which serve this purpose rather well – Zechariah, Isaiah, Daniel, Micah, Matthew, and Revelations. In a bizarre story, the 7th chapter of Daniel is among the most enlightening, yet alarming. In it, there is an end time, political / religious power-house which is *"exceedingly strong"* or in other words with global influence like no other before. This is the impending "New World Order Beast" which is upon us. In conjunction with other prophetic books, particularly the book of Revelations, we can see that this world political power-house ultimately gives rise to the dragon, which is Satan or the Anti-Christ. Incidentally, these books were deemed "harmless" by the religious authorities long ago because their symbolic and prophetic content was not known then.

What is the new role of the now somewhat centrist and at times even leftist Vatican? First of all, no other religious or political power-house today has the world-wide clout of the Vatican. When the pope talks, people listen – in particular people in power, politicians, dictators, presidents, and prime-ministers. We see her (the Church) wealthier and stronger than ever; having an impact on the whole world. She is by far the most revered of all. With more political muscle than any country, her lands are declared off- limits to any foreign military power as she rises above all governing authority. Chapter 17 of the book of Revelations describes her quite eloquently. She is the *"great harlot"* that the kings of the earth have committed (political) fornication with. She has many ultra- wealthy friends in high places and great financial clout throughout the world. She is declared in verse 5 as *"Babylon, the great mother of harlots"* – more on Babylon in chapter 8. It even reveals the geographic "headquarters" of this political super-whore in verse 9 – amidst seven mountains – or Rome. Interesting to note that, in the middle of the seven mountains, one finds the "head" of the global religious-political-financial establishment.

Revelations 18:3, *"Far all nations have drunk the wine of her impure passion, and the kings of the earth have committed fornication with her, and the merchants of the earth have grown rich with the wealth of her wantonness."*

From Rome then, the beast/Anti-Christ will rise with all power and glory as Christ himself deceiving the masses and causing even fire to come down from heaven-Rev 13:13. As was the dress-code of ancient Babylonian high priests is the pope's personification, aura, and wardrobe (ie: his mitre, or headdress which reads "Vicarius Filii Dei"). This beast/Anti-Christ will force his "mark" – the infamous "number of a man" on humanity (as a cat "sprays" to mark his territory) [# 666 – Rev 13:16-18]. Some churches teach this Anti-Christ will be Muslim, however, they lack any substantial reasoning, nor is there a feasible explanation as to why "his number" is not revealed or correlated to their explanation. This Anti-Christ could be a false Jew in the Vatican (ie: "Roman-Jew"). Whatever the case, Satan, being the impostor, will proclaim to be the true "Messiah Christ."

As other languages do, a numeric value is given to letters of the alphabet; the original Roman Numerals were :

I	V	X	L	C	D	
1	5	10	50	100	500	= 666

LUDOVICUS = Vicar of the COURT-

L	U	D	O	V	I	C	U	S	
50	5	500	0	5	1	100	5	0	= 666

DUX CLERI – Captain of the Clergy.

D	U	X	C	L	E	R	I	
500	5	10	100	50	0	0	1	= 666

THE PAPACY

VICARIUS FILII DEI is the formal Latin title of "His Holiness", which means substituting or in the place of the Son of God. In a translation from its own roman 'numerology':

V= 5	F=0	D=500
I=1	I=1	E=0
C=100	L=50	I=1
A=0	I=1	———
R=0	I=1	501
I=1	———	
U=5	53	
S =0		
———		
112		

112 + 53 + 501 = 666 {# 666} = "The Mark of the Beast"
(Note: The "U" and the "V" were used interchangeably by Rome)
*The Beast = the coming world government which will be under control of the apostate Church in unison with many other faiths and

peoples except the "saints." This political / religious powerhouse will persecute these saints who refuse to include other deities as will become mandatory (Revelations 13:7).

*The mark = giving homage to the "image" / idol / embodiment which represents the beast (Revelation 13:15). This is a colossal violation of the first and second commandments. Economic factor of "the mark": Revelation 13:16-17, *"Also it causes all, both small and great, both rich and poor, both free and slave, to be marked on the right hand or the forehead , so that no one can buy or sell unless he has the mark...."* This clearly brings the religious factor and the financial factor into one, giving clear and convincing evidence that the financial world powers and their religious counterparts will be "One." This is likely to come about as a culmination of the present "war on terrorism" which could warrant a move toward a cash-less society as well as a unification of all gods / religions for the sake of "saving mankind." Those who are "free" may not be limited to those who live in a free and democratic society but also those who will be free of debt. Those who will be "slaves" could also be they who are enslaved to debt not just those who are modern day slaves or those who are incarcerated.

By adhering to the "all faith embracing" edicts of the apostate Roman Catholic Church's new age brand of right-wing dominated ideology, political / legal and social mandates, and the Roman-Gregorian festivals spoken of earlier, one will be "in hot water" spiritually as the beast makes his infamous "mark" of apostasy in the forehead (ideology, worship) and / or [right] hand (actions based on the ideology, worship).

*The "nucleus" of the evil mark {#666}, then, is primarily centered around the first and second commandments which deal with idolatry, for God himself explicitly states "I am a jealous God" (Exodus 20:5)- and Satan knows this all too well. By violating the first two, one would also be breaking the third, since the inclusion of other gods makes vile use of the true name of God. The fourth commandment, having to do with time, would be a secondary element of the mark. The sum of the mark is made up of the most comprehensive violation of the first four commandments (mind you, the only ones which have to do with the relationship between God and man – the other six are between man and man).

Through the thousands of masks of evil, Satan will in effect draw many to his "politically correct," yet completely diabolical / Anti-Christ NWO system. That final mask he will deceive many Jews, Christians, Muslims and others with will be the donning of the face of Christ – thus, Satan will save the best for last.

SELECTED CREDITS

J.R. Church & Gary Stearman, *"The Mystery of the Menorah."* Oklahoma City, Oklahoma: Prophesy Publications, 1993.

REVELATIONS 17 -
THE KINGS OF THE EARTH COMMIT{POLITICAL} FORNICATION
WITH "THE HARLOT" (VATICAN):

The Associated Press, Angela Charlton, *"Pope Visits Soviet Union,"* November 9, 1999.

J.M. Dawson Institute of Church-State Studies, Dr. Nikolas K. Gvosdev, *"Pope's Visit to India Highlights Global Rise in Religious Intolerance,"* November 10, 1999.

Time Magazine, Richard N. Ostling / New York and Greg Burke / Rome, *"The Pope Lays Plans For a Trip to Iraq,"* June 29,1998.

Yahoo News, *"Iraq Newspaper says Pope is Welcome,"* Thursday, July 1, 1999.

The Tampa Tribune, John Tagliabue of The New York Times, *"Vatican Planning for Majestic Millennium,"* Sunday, January 24, 1999.

Washington Post Report, *"Catholic Church Takes Political Role in Mexico,"* 1999.

The Associated Press, Victor L. Simpson, *"Pope Entertains Italy's New Leader, An Ex-Communist Party Boss,"* Saturday, January 9,1999.

The Associated Press, *"Pope Visits With Fidel Castro,"* Sunday December 27, 1998.

The New York Times, Alessandra Stanley, *"Pope Visits Ukraine to Fix Orthodox Rift,"* Sunday, June 24, 2001.

The New York Times, Melinda Henneberger, *"Pope Calls for Peaceful Resolution,"* Astana, Kazakhstan, Sunday, September 23, 2001.

St Petersburg Times / Associated Press, *"Pope Declares Chinese Saints, Angers*

Beijing, " Monday, October 2, 2000.

The Tampa Tribune / Associated Press, *"Pius IX Beatification Stirs Epic Debate,"* Sunday, September 3, 2000.

Time 100: Leaders and Revolutionaries, *"Pope John Paul II,"* 1999.

Malachi Martin, *"The Keys of This Blood."* New York: Simon & Schuster, 1990. {The Pope as International Geo-Political Leader, P.490}

"Ludovicus" was proposed by James Bicheno (d. 1831), a British minister and author.

"Dux Cleri" is cited by Walter Brute, a fourteenth century follower of Wycliff, in his Registrum, p.356.

[# 666] – *"The Number of the Beast,"* {also explained in Greek and Hebrew www.aloha.net%7Emikesch/666.html}

The Institute of Religious Knowledge, *"The Illuminati 666."* Brushton, New York: Teach Services, 1983.

[# 666] – Taught at numerous "Protestant Churches."

CHAPTER SEVEN

BABYLON / EGYPT
Historically and Prophetically

For a number of reasons, I believe the fallen angels had a hand in the making of the Egyptian pyramids, as well as Machupichu, Peru and other unexplained phenomena. These were "the mighty men of old" who had great physical strength and advanced intelligence (ie: Egyptian and Greek "mythology"). These fallen angels or demons were also known as "Nephilim." Genesis 6:4, *"The Nephilim were on the earth in those days, and also afterward, when the sons of God came into the daughters of men, and they bore children to them. These were the mighty men that were of old, the men of renown."* Because of the resulting genetic mix between human women and the fallen angels, God sent the great and terrible flood which killed the half-human, half-demonic generation(s). Satan and his fallen angels, however, were not done away with then – if they had been, we would be living in "paradise" now.

These demons initialized the worship of many gods, particularly the sun and the stars. It is a fact that the triangle, too, was honored long ago by pagans, as the number three is symbolic of magic, astrology, and divination. As many know, the science of astronomy has always played and will play a pivotal role during "the last days" as there will be many "signs in the skies"(ie: full moons, meteor showers, falling stars). The three wise men knew of Christ's birth via astronomy, not astrology. It is crucial that the reader understand another "flip flop" – Satan turned a celestial science, astronomy, into a diabolic science: astrology. As Stevie Wonder recited in one of his famous songs, *"When you believe in things you don't understand, then you suffer."* Long ago, the Sumerians built ziggurats (large towers shaped like pyramids) which were dedicated to any one of the variety of false gods they believed in. These were as shrines to appease the gods, of which the "top dog" was Re, or again, the sun god. The Babylonian / Egyptian gods were the idols which Satan used to have dominion over those who were "marked" in their foreheads – hence, the Roman connection (see oracle about Egypt -Isaiah 19; caution to those who rely on Egypt – Isaiah 31). The Sumerians, as many today, believed in unifying that which is of this world with the celestial world (Campell, p.82).

It is my conclusion that mankind has not been explained these mysteries (ie: Atlantis, UFO's) not because no one knows, but because this would "open a can of worms" like no other – exposing some of the secrets of the hierarchies and their works of evil. Since the modern day Bible only holds a fragment of the "whole truth" and we are in essence missing the rest, we have only that coupled with archaeology to shed light on many mysteries. John 20:30, *"Now Jesus did many other signs in the presence of the disciples which are not written in this book."* The fascinating science of archaeology has indeed sided with much of Biblical doctrine as they discover and uncover more of the treasures which the earth has swallowed up. A striking fact is that even scientists are becoming convinced of the reality that the ancient Hebrew texts coincide with recent findings.

The Old Testament reveals a peculiarity which is also quite relevant for today – Egypt as she was spiritually, is who she is today (not the country, as will be explained in the other half of this chapter). Repeatedly, God is commanding that his people "exit- Egypt" – or in other words to separate themselves from what Egypt represented back then, the epicenter for wickedness. We see this theme throughout the Old Testament because God has always been opposed to the idol-centered and wicked ways found in Babylon / Egypt. What Egypt represented was often on the diabolic end of the spectrum, and, therefore, was and is a haven for Satanic activity and pagan gods made of gold. It is from here that all forms of witchcraft, sorcery, necromancy, and the likeness of all evil transcended to the rest of the world. As servants of the Grand Dragon (Satan), the Pharaohs were themselves the embodiment of evil. They were kings who ruled the land by consulting with mediums, astrologers, and seers (ie: as in the days of "voo-doo politics" which Ronald and Nancy Reagan became well known for). We are all familiar with the arrogant Pharaoh who provoked the One True God of Moses, and the fact that he epitomized what it meant to be "wicked to the bone"- hence, the ten plagues of Egypt.

In "coming out of Egypt," God blessed his people then as he does now. As one separates himself from Egypt, he or she separates from the evil which is intertwined with this world. To 'come out of her' is to come clean, to be redeemed, to be at one with God. (Yom Kippur, or the Hebrew "Day of Atonement," is a reminder to those believing Jews and Christians that Christ's blood takes us out of Egypt and makes us "at one" with his Father. It is through Christ's blood that we are atoned for and delivered from this world.)

WHAT, WHERE, WHO IS BABYLON / EGYPT NOW?
As has been for millennia, Satan has come in sheep's clothing doing good to those who follow his "imperialist edicts." Since nothing good lies in the demonic realm, whatever good it does is with mal intent in the long run. It will handsomely enrich those who serve its purposes and objectives. This gives a very clear explanation as to why many a crooked, heartless, and dirty person only gains more, while many of the good and righteous get run over more and more in this evil world. Therefore, it is very important that one realize that oftentimes good can come from bad, as it is essential for evil to do and appear positive and good in order to get the negative and bad results it always seeks. From an economic standpoint, this modern day Egypt is "deregulating" and "privatizing" America, among many other nations, slowly, but surely. The average American is being deceived into believing that the numerous "friendly mergers" (a more appropriate term might be "takeovers") are really to their benefit. Fact is, they are the truest form of what constitutes a "national security threat"- even more than the threat of terrorism. Any monetary surpluses which

the U.S. had just a couple of years ago are now history. This is to this country's detriment in every sense of the word, but since it is primarily an international right-wing conspiracy, many will not "see the train until it's too late." As Matthew 24:39 says, *"and they did not know until the flood came and swept them all away, so will be the coming of the Son of man."* Egypt is a term which prophetically refers to a last day universal hierarchy that gives homage to the same idolatry and wickedness of yesterday. Thus, Egypt is everywhere, in every country; it is the sum total of all countries brought together by a globalist hierarchy using both extreme right and extreme left conspiracies, with the right as the overbearing force. It is this Egypt who is bringing about acceptance for that which is not righteous, hatred toward that which is good, and flipping everything "upside down." Thus, Egypt will again persecute God's people as she did in the past – by condemning those who follow God / Christ, the One True God, the One True Christ.

This multi-national conglomerate of states today is headed by the United Nations, the headquarters of the communist-socialist New World Order (NWO). Originally, The League of Nations, the U.N. has been transformed into a modern day "pantheon." Its "Meditation Room" is actually designed for the worship of any deity or goddess which is in direct conflict with the first commandment of Exodus 20. This NWO group, however, is not for equal distribution of the world's wealth, but it is the utmost of capitalists, with nothing less than total global economic control among its top goals. It was born of pantheists, occultists (encompasses a variety, such as the freemasons / masons who incidentally own the "inauguration Bible"), secularists, and the multi-billion dollar European trans-nationalist banking cartels who are the muscle behind the "Beast" (aka: The Council on Foreign Relations and the Trillateral Commission / IMF and World Bank). They are all secret-societies made up primarily of mega-wealthy organizations with close ties to the Vatican who is at the center of this diabolic goal of creating a "New Age Inter- Faith Global Society." This process, known as "syncresis" (Malachi Martin, p 299), will in essence enmesh good and evil into one.

Since the true Christ cannot be of this group, this explains why the evil empire must create the apostate or false Christianity spoken of earlier. The changed policy of the now "inclusive and humanist" Vatican in conjunction with the gradual modification of other faiths and its world-wide political clout allows for the integration of most, if not all nations, religions, traditions, beliefs, and cultures under the auspices of the U.N..

The Federal Reserve, which is not a public entity (as in controlled "by the people") as many Americans are led to believe, is in itself an enigma of sorts. Controlled by the globalists and their colleagues, this highly polished group of international banking hierarchies have many a "skeleton in the closet." To some degree, these "secrets" actually make a mockery of the American people at large as so many believe that "In God We Trust." What they have not explained is which God they really refer to – the one described by the Apostle Paul in 2 Corinthians 4:4: *"In their case the god of this world has blinded the minds of the unbelievers, to keep them from seeing the light of the gospel of the glory of Christ, who is the likeness of God."* (Note: Christ is the "lamb of God." He is like God. He is not God. Yahweh is God.) It certainly gives a viable explanation as to why the architecture of some U.S. Government buildings mimics that found in Rome / Babylon and why there is an obelisk in Washington D.C.. Even more peculiar is the hexagram (aka: Star of David which is not Biblical) made up of thirteen stars enclosed in a "solar disk" and the mysterious pyramid on our dollar bill with "the all seeing eye" of Horus, son of Isis and Osiris (which as mentioned earlier, is also the logo for some corporations) – with the Latin inscription "Novus Ordo Seclorem" or New Secular Order / New World Order. The mere fact that this is written in Latin reveals the profound authority of the conservative Church of this new age as ever-present and all-so-dominating. The sun deities spoken of previously are also inculcated into the dollar bill as we see the solar eagle, which is "the bird and vehicle of Zeus" (Campell, p.125). Zeus, like Hercules, was another fallen angel. This is the ultimate "pyramid scheme." It is no coincidence that Abraham Lincoln, who left his "liberal legacy" is the President who got to be on the U.S. penny, the least valuable coin. Note: Though my research has led me to the realization that the Star of David / Seal of Solomon is pagan in origin, I am not implying that those who honor it are necessarily wicked – as is the case with those who venerate idols, ignorance is the issue. Then there's the Miami-Dade "Raelians" who promote cloning – they too, integrate the star into their beliefs. It is worth noting that in Rome, specifically St. Peter's Square at the Vatican, there is also an obelisk. As a phallic symbol of Osiris, the obelisk was actually transplanted from Egypt in furthering the acclimation of the nefarious Babylonian culture and symbolism to Rome. The sphinx's of Egypt and the very term "Catholic" are ironically interwoven in the very term CAT-HOLI-C or Holy-Cat. The only "Holy-Cat" is Jesus Christ who is the "Lion of Judah."

Today's "Revived Rome" is in essence attempting to accomplish the very same objective of those who united in a one-world-order, if you will, at the tower-of- Babel (Genesis11:4). The premise was the same then as now: mankind can produce his own pathway to heaven on earth in the absence of God, if only he unites in a common bond. We know that this did not go well with God, as it is impossible for man to accomplish such a feat without him. The world-wide-web is, to a great extent, the globalists attempt to undo the "communication breakdown" which God sent upon mankind. The internet can also be used by God to further the work of spreading the good news to the masses. Thus, it is not necessarily evil.

The Order of the Illuminati or the enlightened order- an offshoot of the Vatican – founded by Dr.Adam Weishaupt who attracted many to his political movement called "Republicanism," has been fervently working for a border-less world which does not seem very far away. It was his secret plan over two hundred years ago to conceal from the masses the "conspiracy" of all conspiracies which is very much alive today particularly within the right-wing of international politics. With the Vatican now having diplomatic ties to over 170 nations, it appears the plan is well under way (ref: National Geographic, "Inside the Vatican", 2001).

We have seen, for example, that the NAFTA and GATT treaties were among some of the stepping stones to this New World Order, not to mention the creation of the World Trade Organization (WTO) and of course, the European Union (EU). The world is more inter-dependent than ever. This was evident during the financial break-down of some Asian and South American countries, not to mention the potential delicate scenario unfolding in the Mid-East. The *"desolating of sacrilege"* (which prophesies of a religious and po-litical take-over of "the holy place") will arise from the imminent intervention on the part of the Anti-Christ himself – via the U.N. or a new global entity yet to be formed- Matthew 24:15. Factoid: The E.U. contributes more money to the U.N. than even the U.S – Holtje, p.207. This could feasibly occur sooner than later as the Far-Right in Israel sparks up flames of passion resulting from their false sense of what is fair, just, and "right." Has their "state-sponsored terrorism," particularly in the recent past, been all that different from other forms of terrorism? The Jews in Israel and throughout the world who have protested the oppression of the Palestinian people deserve greater acknowledgement and praise. The hard right-wingers of this world have greatly added fuel to this incendiary situation which will inad-vertently make things even worse as they rise with great brutal force seeking to "balance the scales of justice" (which only God and Christ can really do).

In recent decades, we have seen the mammoth influence of the globalists as many presidents and foreign heads of state have en-dorsed and applauded both the NWO and the U.N.. The "new age" modern cults, being an integral part of this NWO, which is an off-shoot of the Church, are not new at all. They are the satanists, kabba-lists, occultists, freemasons, gnostics, eastern mystics, necromancers, magicians, wiccans, wizards, witches, numerologists, voo-doo priests, santeria and brujería priests, soothsayers, astrologers (not astrono-mers), fortune tellers, seers, 1-900 psychics, pagans, palm, and tarot readers of yesterday. They are now looked upon as legitimate spir-itual partners of the same God by the U.N., among others. The ex-treme leftists within the above stated list are ultimately "swallowed up" by the mighty Far-Right which, again, has a diverse face of in-clusion, compassion, and kindness, but a mind polluted with racist, imperialist, and fascist objectives. There is just no doubt that the manner in which the right-wing political and religious establishment manipulates much of the left, as we have seen throughout previous chapters, is of huge proportions. This is why the U.S. economy, Constitution, and legal system are on a dangerous path toward further globalist influence on an unseen scale and at a very rapid pace. One could say these days: "The Europeans are coming, the Europeans are coming."

Cleverly, the demonic realm has made sure that enough of the earth's inhabitants would be led astray in making a last ditch effort to unify man into its all faith embracing world government where "it's all good" – a very popular cliche today. If one believes in Christ, he or she must never forget that although he embraces all peoples, he does not embrace all philosophy, thus all is [not] good.

Long before the Ten Commandments were given to Moses, there existed a code of laws by the famous Babylonian lawgiver, Hammurabi. Although they were quite elaborate and in some cases similar to the Hebrew law, they were not of the One True God, thus, not perfectly fair or just (ie: the death penalty was allowed for one who committed certain property related crimes), but nevertheless considered good and righteous. If it was truly good, there would not have arisen the need for the Hebrew doctrine via Moses. Since the fallen angels had a "celestial education" they governed in the only way they knew how –a way that originated in the heavens, hence, why previous cultures and doctrines had striking similarities.

For eons, man, through Satan's influence, has flipped things "upside down," rationalizing that what he alone perceives as good is good because his infantile intelligence concludes it is – Proverbs 16:25: *"There is a way that seemeth right unto a man, but the end thereof are the ways of death."* And every single time he has done the "flip-flop" he has paid a dear price for going too far in his strive toward complete autonomy from his maker which often results in the inclusion of foreign gods, as was common in Egypt. 1 Corinthians 10: 22: *"You can not drink the cup of the Lord and the cup of demons"* – why? Because either one is on one team or on the other, for there is not a third "party" one can join by denouncing the two – what is interesting is that if one were to denounce the two, he would simply be classified as being on Satan's side, for anything against

God / Christ is deemed evil. In Matthew 12: 30, Christ sums it up this way: *"He who is not with me is against me, and he who does not gather with me scatters."* Declaring someone "evil," again, is ultimately for God to make; we who are true followers of Christ are to refrain, as is possible, from judging others. Because we are all evil to some extent, the Apostle Paul wrote, *"be babes in evil"* (1 Corinthians 14:20).

The scriptures are clear: either one's name will be "written in the book of life" or it will not, either one will come *"out of Egypt"* or he/she will not (Rev 20:11-13). The ancient practices and rituals of Babylon / Egypt are very much in every corner of the globe today, which serves as verification that the whole world is now "Egypt."

So it is very true that since "Satan is divided against himself" his time is ticking and will eventually fall by his own doings. It is human nature to repeat the same mistakes of the past, for the wickedness, haughtiness, and hardness of heart which were so commonplace during the days of Noah, are everywhere today. Though the end may or may not be right around the bend (the signs of the times do warrant swift celestial intervention on a grand scale and are in line with what would precede the end of days / "coming of the Son of man" in Biblical prophecy), it surely will mirror the end which befell on mankind during the days of Noah: *"But of that day and hour no one knows, not even the angels of heaven, nor the Son of man, but the Father only. As it was in the days of Noah, so it will be at the coming of the Son of Man"* (Matthew 24:36-37). In a final attempt at creating a NWO and a false and misleading last day universal Christian Church, Satan will use every trick in the book before his end "draweth nigh"- and his book of tricks is lengthy. Ezekiel 28:11-20 explains vividly the story of Satan, from beginning to end.

SELECTED CREDITS

Chuck Missler, *"Return of the Nephilim"* vidoetape, 1997.

Associated Press Report, *"1999 Offers A Rare Succession of Full Moons Not Seen in 80 Years,"* Friday January 1,1999.

E. W. Bullinger, *"The Witness of the Stars."* Grand Rapids, MI: Kregel Publications, 2000. {Astronomy}

George Hart, *Dictionary of Egyptian Gods and goddesses*, 1996.

Joseph Campell, *"The Mythic Image."* Princeton, NJ: Princeton University Press, 1974. {Marriage of Heaven and Earth}

Bob Anderson, *"Foreshocks of Anti-Christ."* Eugene, Oregon: Harvest House Publishers, 1997. {The Reagan's and Astrology, p.88}

International Herald Tribune, Guy Gugliotta of the Washington Post, *"Black Sea Discovery Evokes Biblical Story of Noah,"* Paris, France, Thursday, September 14, 2000.

John C. Whitcome, *"The World that Perished."* Grand Rapids, MI: Baker Book House, 1988. {Archaeology and The Bible}

Malachi Martin, *"The Keys of this Blood."* New York: Simon & Schuster, 1990. {The Pope as World Leader / "Syncresis"}

New York Times, Barbara Crosette, *"New Anxiety Over Idea of a Borderless Justice,"* Monday, July, 2, 2001.

Dr. James W. Wardner, D.M.D., *"The Planned Destruction of America."* DeBary, Fl: Longwood Communications, 1994. {International Banking Cartels / One World Order}

The Institute for Religious Knowledge, *"The Illuminati 666."* Brushton, New York: Teach Services, 1983. {Dr Adam Weishaupt / One World Order / One Dollar Bill}

Newswatch Magazine, Jean Kirkpatrick, *"Bush Pushes Global view,"* May-June, 1991. www.newswatchmagazine.org

Newswatch Magazine, *"To Communize-Socialize Amerika,"* November 15, 1997. www.newswatchmagazine.org

Democratic National Committee, *"Bush Erases Budget Surplus,"* Friday, September 7, 2001.

American Free Press Magazine, *"For Life and Liberty / Against the New World Order,"* www.americanfreepress.net

J.R. Church, *"Guardians of the Grail."* Oklahoma City, OK: Prophesy Publications, 1989. {The Illuminati / The United States of Europe}

Gary H. Kah, *"The New World Religion."* Noblesville, Indiana: Hope International Publishing, 1998. {The Vatican and the United Nations}

The Spotlight Newspaper, James P. Tucker Jr., *"Media Spotlight Shines On Bilderberg,"* Stenungsund, Sweden – Volume XXVII, Number 23, June 4, 2001. www.spotlight.org

Elisabeth Goldsmith, *"Ancient Pagan Symbols."* New York: G. P. Putnams and Sons, 1929. {The Six-Pointed Star / Hexagram, pp144-146}

Gershom Scholem, *"On the Kabbalah and it's Symbolism."* New York: Schoken Books, 1996.

The Hex, The Star of David, With quotes from Gershom Scholem's book, *"The Star of David,"* www.jesus-messiah.com/apologetics/jewish/star-of-david.html

South Florida Sun-Sentinel, James D. Davis, *"Raelians Believe Cloning Leads To An Eternal Life,"* Sunday September 23, 2001.

Joseph Campell, *"The Inner Reaches of Outer Space."* New York: Harper and Row Publishers, 1986. {Solar Eagle}

Stanley Meisler, *"United Nations, The First Fifty Years."* New York: The Atlantic Monthly Press, 1995.

Collier's Encyclopedia, *"United Nations,"* Great Britain: The Crowell-Collier Publishing Co., 1963. {"The Meditation Room" Volume 22, P.648}

James Holtje, *"Divided it Stands: Can the United Nations Work?"* Atlanta, Georgia: Turner Publishing, Inc. 1995.

The Associated Press, *"The Pope's U.N. visit,"* 1996.

Yahoo News / The Associated Press, Dina Kraft, *"Israel Welcomes Pope Statement,"* Wednesday, June 30,1999.

St. Petersburg Times, *"Proposal gives U.N. control of Holy sites,"* September, 2000.

The Christian Science Monitor, Ilene R. Prusher, *"Israeli Media Shifts to the Right,"* Tuesday, October 16, 2001.

International Herald Tribune, *"60 Israeli Veterans Refuse to Serve: Petition by Reservists Condemns West Bank and Gaza Occupation,"* Paris, France, January 29, 2002.

Gershon Salomon, *"Israel Training Sanhedrin Again,"* August 8, 2000. www.endtimeinfo.net/temple/sanhedrin.html

"The Anti-Christ Will Set Himself Up In The Temple as God" – A revelation which many Protestant denominations concur with. www.cynet.com/jesus/prophesy/setup.html

PROFILES OF CHRIST AND CONCLUSION

Though it is clear that the more commonly held view to many is that of a conservative-rightist Jesus Christ, to some he is a liberal sort of Messiah. There are those who see the "leftist" side of Christ, one who does not necessarily fit the mold which the masses see. To peer into the scriptures and "read between the lines" one finds numerous excerpts portraying a humble, forgiving, compassionate, gentle, humanitarian, inclusive (of all people – not of other gods), tolerant, caring, and loving Messiah – again, not terms which have been an integral part of the Far-Right. The Far-Right, on the other hand, has been arrogant, harsh, condemning, barbaric, hate-filled, racist, unforgiving, and very uncompassionate – basically the opposite of Christ. This mindset is the same yesterday and today, however, now it is cloaked in "political correctness." Throughout the New Testament, we find that Christ's aura was not at all in line with many conservatives of those days – or these days. He, as his true followers, was as a devil to the political system and to many V.I.P.'s of those times – particularly, the know-it-all Scribes and Pharisees who had a variety of similarities in terms of their self-righteous attitudes to many of today's hard right-wingers. Curiously, it was in heated dialogues with these two groups that we see the very essence of Christ's sovereignty over and above their ridiculous earthly views which were much too hypocritical and judgmental. In many instances these Scribes and Pharisees were out to condemn and trap Christ in his sayings and doings, but not once were they successful, for they were likened to

"Synagogues of Satan" – wicked, heartless, and full of conceit, holding to the power of religion while ignoring the weightier matters of life. Jeremiah 5:26, *"For wicked men are found among my people; they lurk like fowlers lying in wait. They set a trap; they catch men."* Christ used a higher justice than ours, to make nothing the ways of this world, and to edify those of the next.

To look at the sort of constant misunderstanding between his philosophy and that of the Scribes and Pharisees, one can conclude two very basic points. First, his messages would not be hard to decipher if one lent an ear to what the spirit was saying. The second is the fact that so many did not understand the moral of his parables because they were too engulfed in the precepts of their earthly views thus could not rise above that plane of consciousness and grasp a higher knowledge, superior wisdom, and true justice. When one is so full of himself or herself, how can he or she hear the spirit of God? Could it be that he or she may not only be wrong, but that others, oftentimes those we least expect, may be right? Some of the "lowly" of this world were, are, and will be much more aligned with God than many of those who profess a oneness with him only to be praised by men.

Christ took various opportunities to demonstrate that he, as his Father, takes both liberal and conservative positions depending on the circumstances at hand. Let's examine a few key examples:

a) Did Christ allow the temple to be used as a locale for money changers? Absolutely not. He threw them out in a heartbeat! – his conservative end. Clearly, this is an example of when not to "turn the other cheek."

b) Did Christ instruct his flock to be generous, kind, and goodhearted with one another? A resounding yes. He was totally opposed to being "hard of heart" and "cold as ice" – again a position which revealed a more liberal tone.

c) Was it lawful to do good on the Sabbath? The more conservative crowd thought absolutely not. The liberal side of Christ confronted their earthly views, making fools of them by revealing that the law granted priority to the more important issues of life, as in prioritizing in order to do what is truly righteous or good (ie: healing the sick, feeding the hungry, clothing the naked).

d) Did Christ promote the Ten Commandments his Father had given Moses? Absolutely. When it came to his Father's ten general rules of conduct for the Israelites, Christ was primarily conservative – even more-so with the first three.

Christ took, takes, and will take from either left or right what he sees fit in order to execute a perfect justice and to synchronize the scales of righteousness like no worldly government has ever done. Today's hard-line Scribes, Pharisees, and adherents are everywhere, and Christ's penetrating and provocative parables are as applicable in the year 2000 as they were in his day. To observe the same tenet two hundred years apart or two thousand does not change one iota in any way whatsoever simply because man at his core does not change either. We are no different than Adam and Eve. Neither does the philosophy, ethics, or morale of the celestial body change.

CONCLUSION

From the traditional Roman Catholic Church to the modernized, all inclusive Vatican of today, one can sense that there are more than just a couple of reasons why the political framework and religious customs of the "New-Church" have been reshaping this world-wide geo-political power-house into what is a partly leftist organization. Simply put, the objective is to have sovereignty over all peoples through one massive World Government ruled by the Anti-Christ. The U.N. may very well undergo a reform or even be replaced in order for the final New World Order to be ushered in. This aim at total sovereignty is the work of Satan and his crew, as his last show of strength, before he is finally defeated by Christ.

The story of the wide-path and the narrow path in the New Testament may be most applicable in the present than at any time before in the history of mankind, for it is now that the masses are more educated, thus, have an improved ability to reason. The wide path is where the ways of the world are, the narrow where the ways of God are. The narrow path of God includes peoples of all races, but not other gods; it includes, yet excludes. Throughout the Bible as we have seen, there is talk about the right and the left, and that we, as children of God, should adhere and remember that to lean too far to either side is to step into the wide path. There is room for leaning to one side or the other depending on the circumstance at hand, thus, we would do well to see what the Bible says – from a modestly liberal perspective as well as a mildly conservative one. It is there that we find when to have leniency and when to be stern. It is there that a higher justice prevails. When one deviates toward extremist ideology, one is essentially going against God Almighty, Jesus Christ, and The Ten Commandments, plus the eleventh one to "love one another."

The Ten Commandments which were placed in the *"Ark of the Covenant"* (Genesis 50:26) also have prophetic significance which is described in Rev.11:15-19: *"Then the seventh angel blew his trumpet, and there were loud voices in heaven, saying, "The kingdom of the world has become the kingdom of our Lord and of his Christ and he shall reign for ever and ever. And the twenty four elders who sit on their thrones fell on their faces and worshipped God, saying, 'We give thanks to thee Lord God Almighty, who art and who wast, that thou hast taken thy great power and begun to reign. The nations raged, but thy wrath came and the time for the dead to be judged, for rewarding thy servants, the prophets and saints, and those who fear thy name, both small and great, and for destroying the destroyers of the earth.' Then God's temple in heaven was opened and the ark of his covenant was seen within his temple; and there were flashes of lightning, voices, peals of thunder, an earthquake, and heavy hail."*

The following passage, though it can be interpreted in other ways, may shed some light on the overall theme of this book and the numerous Biblical excerpts mentioned earlier which relate in some way or another to the center: Matthew 7:13 -14 – " *Enter by the narrow gate; for the gate is wide and the way is easy that leads to destruction, and those who enter by it are many. For the gate is narrow and the way is hard that leads to life, and those who find it are few."* The narrow gate, being synonymous with following Christ's many examples, is where justice, faith, mercy, love, humility, generosity, compassion, and human warmth are.

As the wavy lines below separate the modest from the radical, the narrow path becomes distinct from the wide:

9 8 7 6 5 4 3 2 1 0 **I** 0 1 2 3 4 5 6 7 8 9

EVIL~~~~~~~~ * ————RIGHTEOUS————* ~~~~~~~EVIL

[those who classify an 8 or 9 may certainly want to rethink their radical views.]

```
WIDE PATH            narrow              WIDE PATH
EXTREME LEFT                           EXTREME RIGHT
RADICAL             MODEST                  RADICAL

I~~~~~~~~~~~~~~*———————c—————*~~~~~~~~~~~~~~~~I
```

Throughout the writings of the Apostle Paul, it is more than clear that to be modest is one of his primary messages. To be modest is to be more inclined toward the middle, to be less / non-judgmental, to be humane, to love your brother as yourself, to be "evenly balanced."

We should keep in mind that the vast majority of conservative Biblical theology portrays sin as being synonymous with the left, but, as this book has explained, the Bible itself has quite a bit to say regarding sin which is synonymous with the right. 2 Corinthians 6:14-16 – *"Come out from among them, and be ye separate...and touch not the unclean...and ...I will receive you , and will be a Father unto you, and ye shall be my sons and daughters, sayeth the Lord Almighty."*

Joshua 24: 23 – *"Then put away the foreign gods which are among you, and incline your heart to the Lord, the God of Israel."* By doing so, one becomes a "novus homo" (new man / woman).

May the One True God **Yahweh** bless you and remember that Jesus Christ's 'element of surprise' will bring about the ultimate swift and final judgement of all judgements: Psalms 9:7-8, *"But the Lord sits enthroned for ever, he has established his throne for judgement; and he judges the world with righteousness, he judges the peoples with equity."*

Acts 17:31,*"The times of ignorance God overlooked, but now he commands all men everywhere to repent, because he has fixed a day on which he will judge the world in righteousness by a man whom he has appointed, and of this he has given assurance to all men by raising him from the dead."*

1 Thessalonians 5:2, *"For you yourselves know well that the day of the Lord will come as a thief in the night."*

Revelations 22:13, *"I am the Alpha and the Omega"* –

The One and Only Messiah,
Jesus Christ.

Selah.

Printed in the United States
by Baker & Taylor Publisher Services